DATE DUE

# Rain Forests
## of the
# World

Volume 10
Squirrel–Yanomami People

## MARSHALL CAVENDISH
NEW YORK • LONDON • TORONTO • SYDNEY

Marshall Cavendish Corporation
99 White Plains Road
Tarrytown, New York
10591-9001

Website: www.marshallcavendish.com

Consulting Editors: Rolf E. Johnson, Nathan E. Kraucunas

Contributing Authors:  Theresa Greenaway, Jill Bailey, Michael Chinery, Malcolm Penny, Mike Linley, Philip Steele, Chris Oxlade, Ken Preston-Mafham, Rod Preston-Mafham, Clare Oliver, Don Birchfield

Discovery Books
    Managing Editor: Paul Humphrey
    Project Editor: Gianna Williams
    Text Editor: Valerie Weber
    Designer: Ian Winton
    Cartographer: Stefan Chabluk
    Illustrators: Jim Channell, Stuart Lafford, Christian Webb, Kevin Maddison

Marshall Cavendish
    Editor: Marian Armstrong
    Editorial Director: Paul Bernabeo

*(cover) Golden lion tamarin*

**Editor's Note:** Many systems of dating have been used by different cultures throughout history. *Rain Forests of the World* uses B.C.E. (Before Common Era) and C.E. (Common Era) instead of B.C. (Before Christ) and A.D. (Anno Domini, "In the Year of Our Lord") out of respect for the diversity of the world's peoples.

The publishers would like to thank the following for their permission to reproduce photographs:
548 Terry Whittaker/Frank Lane Picture Agency, 549 Martin Withers/FLPA, 550 Terry Whittaker/FLPA, 551 A. N. T./Natural History Photographic Agency, 552 Mary Plage/Bruce Coleman, 553 Stephen J. Krasemann/Bruce Coleman, 554 Norbert Wu/Oxford Scientific Films, 555 Gerard Lacz/FLPA, 556 Mirko Stelzner/NHPA, 557 John Shaw/NHPA, 558 T. Kitchin & V. Hurst/NHPA, 559 Stephen J. Krasemann/NHPA, 560 Ken Preston-Mafham/Premaphotos Wildlife, 561 Richard Davies/OSF, 562 Terry Whittaker/FLPA, 563 Alain Compost/Bruce Coleman, 564 Corbis, 565 Jeff Foott/Bruce Coleman, 566 Michael Sewell/OSF, 567 Luiz Claudio Marigo/Bruce Coleman, 568 Martin Harvey/NHPA, 569 Micheal Sewell/OSF, 570 Luiz Claudio Marigo/Bruce Coleman, 571 Gerald S. Cubitt/Bruce Coleman, 573 Chris Mattison/FLPA, 574 Gerald S. Cubitt/Bruce Coleman, 575 M. P. L. Fogden/OSF, 576 G. I. Bernard/NHPA, 577 M. P. L. Fogden/Bruce Coleman, 578 Daniel J. Cox/OSF, 579 Gerald S. Cubitt/Bruce Coleman, 580 Harold Taylor ABIPP/OSF, 581 Ken Preston-Mafham/Premaphotos Wildlife, 582 Hans Reinhard/OSF, 583 Deni Brown/OSF, 584 Michael Goulding/Partridge Films Ltd./OSF, 585 Corbis, 586 Hans Reinhard/Bruce Coleman, 587 & 588 Chris Mattison/FLPA, 589 Zig Leszczynski/OSF, 590 George Gainsburgh/NHPA, 591 Michael Fogden/OSF, 594 Marie Read/Bruce Coleman, 595 Ken Preston-Mafham/Premaphotos Wildlife, 596 Michael Sewell/OSF, 597 G. I. Bernard/NHPA, 598 Edward Parker/OSF, 599 Zig Leszczynski/OSF, 600 David Woodfall/NHPA, 602 Ken Preston-Mafham/Premaphotos Wildlife, 603 G. I. Bernard/NHPA, 604 & 605 Jerry Callow/Panos Pictures

**Library of Congress Cataloging-in-Publication Data**
Rain forests of the world.
              v.  cm.
        Includes bibliographical references and index.
        Contents: v. 1. Africa-bioluminescence — v. 2. Biomass-clear-cutting — v. 3. Climate and weather-emergent — v. 4. Endangered species-food web — v. 5. Forest fire-iguana — v. 6. Indonesia-manatee — v. 7. Mangrove forest-orangutan — v. 8. Orchid-red panda — v. 9. Reforestation-spider — v. 10. Squirrel-Yanomami people — v. 11. Index.
              ISBN 0-7614-7254-1 (set)
              1. Rain forests—Encyclopedias. 1. Marshall Cavendish Corporation.
        QH86 .R39 2002
        578.734—dc21

    ISBN 0-7614-7254-1 (set)
    ISBN 0 7614-7264-9 (vol. 10)

Printed and bound in Italy

07 06 05 04 03 02   6 5 4 3 2 1

# Contents

# Squirrel

The familiar squirrel, bright-eyed and bushy-tailed, belongs to a highly adaptable group of animals. Worldwide, 267 species have been named, living in every habitat from semiarid desert to temperate and tropical rain forests.

Squirrels range in size from mouselike pygmy squirrels, found in African forests, to marmots the size of cats. Most live entirely in trees, having sharp claws for climbing and long bushy tails, which they use for steering when they leap among the branches. They are rodents, with sharp incisors (front teeth) that continue to grow throughout their life. Squirrels use them to gnaw tree bark, tough seeds, and nut shells. In rain forests, they feed on a wide variety of foods, from bark and sap to nuts and fruits to insects. Many species eat only leaves, while others eat the growing shoots of young trees. They cause a lot of damage in plantations, where they are regarded as pests. Some tropical squirrels eat only insects. Their front teeth are shaped like tweezers to grip their prey.

In temperate forests and woodlands, squirrels are famous for storing food, burying nuts in autumn to return to them in winter when food is short. This often helps to plant new trees, when the squirrels forget where they left the nuts. In tropical rain forests storing food is unnecessary because there are no seasons and food is available all year round.

*The Douglas squirrel is named for the Douglas firs in the temperate rain forests where it lives.*

## KEY FACTS

● Marmots are large squirrels that live in temperate rain forests.

● Several squirrels can "fly," using gliding membranes stretched between their front and hind legs.

● The giant flying squirrels of the forests of Malaysia can glide as far as 330 ft. (100 m) between trees.

Squirrels breed very quickly and have large families. For this reason they play another important part in the ecology of the forest, providing food for predators such as owls and eagles.

**Flying Squirrels**

The most spectacular squirrels are those that can "fly," using a furry membrane between their front and hind legs that acts like a parachute. Their flight is a gentle downward glide, bringing them down to land on another tree trunk, which they climb up to start the next flight. They steer with their tail, and as they come in to land they lean back so as to stall, losing speed as they hit the target tree. The giant flying squirrels that live in the forests of Malaysia can glide as far as 330 feet (100 m)—about the length of a football field—between trees.

**Feeding the Forest**

The flying squirrels that live in temperate rain forests feed on truffles, strongly scented fungi (FUN-jie) that grow entirely underground. The spores of the truffles are spread in the squirrels' droppings, so wherever squirrels have been, new truffles grow. This explains why truffles have such a strong smell: they need to attract squirrels to dig them up to eat, so that their spores will be spread through the forest. These fungi grow as a fine network, wrapped around the roots of the trees. The fungi take sugars produced by the trees, while they collect minerals from the soil that the tree cannot gather for itself and pass them to the tree. Trees without fungi growing around their roots do not grow as well as those that have them. As the squirrels harvest these fungi and help the fungi reproduce, they are also helping to keep the forest trees healthy.

*IN FOCUS*

## Scaly-Tailed Squirrels

One family, the scaly-tailed squirrels, are only distantly related to the rest. They live in tropical forests in West Africa, gliding among the trees at night. Their tails have a scaly tip that helps them cling to branches. Although they are still quite common, very little is known about them—except that as the old forests where they live are destroyed, they are becoming rarer.

## Check these out:

- Locomotion ● Mammal ● Rodent
- Symbiosis ● Temperate Rain Forest

Subtropical rain forests are really just tropical rain forests growing outside the Tropics, with many of the same plants and animals. Both types of forests are continuous with and blend into each another. Subtropical rain forests grow only where local conditions of climate are suitable for the survival of a warm, moist forest, often protected by nearby mountains or the proximity of warm seas. Subtropical rain forests do, however, sometimes have frosts, which can eliminate certain species of plants and animals that otherwise live happily in tropical forests.

Subtropical rain forests occur in a few places south of the Tropic of Capricorn, which marks the southern boundary of the tropical zone. These forests occur in eastern Australia, southeastern Madagascar, Brazil, Paraguay, and Argentina. In the Northern Hemisphere, north of the line marking the Tropic of Cancer, small areas of subtropical forest push northward into Myanmar, China, and Taiwan.

## KEY FACTS

● **Some of Madagascar's subtropical rain forests are home to 13 species of lemur.**

● **Subtropical rain forests often have even more biting insects than true tropical rain forests.**

● **Unusually severe frosts can damage the wildlife in subtropical rain forests.**

● **Some of Asia's most spectacular butterflies occur only in the subtropical forests.**

*The subtropical Mbaracayu Reserve in Paraguay contains many plants and animals typical of the purely tropical rain forests farther north.*

## Asian Subtropical Forests

The Asian subtropical forests differ from all others because they lie within the monsoon belt. They therefore receive very heavy rainfall on a seasonal basis, breaking a long dry season with a very wet downpour. They end up with some 80 inches (2,000 mm) of rain annually, although some areas receive up to 500 inches (13,000 mm). The forests of Assam in northeast India are particularly wet and lush and have one of the world's richest assemblages of flowering plants. This is the home of such magnificent animals as the Indian one-horned rhinoceros, the hoolock gibbon, giant flying fox fruit bats, hordes of Indian mongooses, and a wide range of interesting squirrels.

## Australian Subtropical Rain Forests

In Australia a lot of interesting examples of subtropical rain forest remain in southern Queensland and northern New South Wales. These forests are dominated by trees such as white beefwood, several kinds of hoop pines, black booyong, crow's ash, rose satinash, blush tulip oak, silky beech, saffron heart (so-named because of its bright yellow wood), and the blood vine, which looks like a huge python coiling around a tree trunk. The scrub bloodwood oozes red sap when cut. This forms an indelible paint once used by the aboriginal people to mark personal items such as bags and blankets. Rose mahogany is a valuable timber tree with a striking, fragrant wood, now largely exterminated from most forests. The leaves and twigs of corkwood were formerly used to catch fish, as they have an intoxicating effect when mashed up and put into water.

# Pademelons

Several kinds of small kangaroos or wallabies inhabit the subtropical rain forests of Australia. One of these is the red-necked pademelon, a miniature kangaroo between 1 and 2 ft. (30 and 60 cm) tall. It eats grass, berries, orchids, and ferns in the deep forest, but it can become very tame and come out to graze on the lawns around tourist lodges. It is active from late afternoon until early morning. Like all kangaroos, it carries its baby in a pouch on its stomach.

Up in the canopy, many of the trees support large spreading bird's nest ferns, which are common epiphytes in these forests. Some of the best of Australia's rain forest areas are now protected in local nature reserves or national parks, but outside these areas destruction continues at a rapid rate.

Many of these forests are home to scrub turkeys. They build large mounds of compost for incubating their eggs by the naturally generated heat of decay. They scratch around on the forest floor for food. The crystal-clear streams that run through the forests are often home to the spectacular blue mountain crayfish, which

lives in holes in the banks and among the roots of the forest trees along the streamsides. Orchids are often present in some numbers, but unlike in most tropical rain forests, where orchids are mainly epiphytic, in these subtropical Australian forests they grow mainly on the ground. The delicate white flowers of the Christmas orchid, so-called because it flowers at Christmastime during the Southern Hemisphere's summer, form elegant drifts on the rain forest floor.

**South American Subtropical Rain Forest**

In South America subtropical rain forests occur along the coast of southeastern Brazil. Some of these forests are still among the most remote and unexplored areas of the continent, cut off from easy access by the sea on one side and steep mountain slopes and gorges on the other. Far away, on the eastern side of the continent, a narrow tongue of forest extends down the base of the Andes mountains into northern Argentina. This forest looks quite different from the tropical forest farther north. Buttressed trees are rare, and many of the branches are heavily festooned with epiphytic plants. Primates are comparatively few, with only two species present, compared with dozens farther north in the truly tropical forests of Amazonia.

The same restriction on primate numbers also applies to the subtropical forest around Iguaçu Falls on the borders of Argentina, Brazil, and Paraguay. Only three kinds of monkeys live in the forests surrounding the mighty falls, which really consist of 275 separate cataracts. Together these generate a permanent 98-foot- (30-m-) high cloud of mist in which multiple rainbows are created by the sun. Swifts dart in and out of the rushing water and even roost on ledges behind the mighty falls themselves.

Up in the canopy toco toucans search for fruits, while on dead trees male toothpick weevils joust with their long lancelike noses for the right to remain on a tree where females are likely to arrive and lay their eggs. Brilliant blue morpho butterflies flit in and out of the glades. This all sounds very much like Amazonia, and in fact much of the life at Iguaçu is the same as found farther north. Yet there is one huge difference between Iguaçu and Amazonia: Iguaçu has a proper winter, during which frosts can cover the ground for a few hours around dawn, making it even more surprising that so many truly tropical creatures thrive there.

## Check these out:

● Asia ● Australia ● Climate and Weather ● Orchid ● Rain Forest ● Season ● South America ● Toucan

# Symbiosis

When two or more different species live together and interact, this is called symbiosis (sim-bee-OE-sis). Symbioses are found throughout the food chain and are vital to the survival of a forest ecosystem.

## Mineral Scavengers

Right at the base of the rain forest food chain, many plants depend upon symbioses with fungi (FUN-jie) or bacteria to survive. The commonest symbiosis in the forest is between the roots of trees, herbs, and ferns, and certain fungi. The fungi may form a net of fine threads around the root, or the fungal threads may penetrate right inside the plant root. The fungi absorb phosphates and other minerals from the soil, which they pass on to the plant. They receive sugars that the plant has made by photosynthesis. These special root-fungus associations are called mycorrhizas.

Bacteria also live in the roots of some plants, especially those of the pea family, which in the Tropics include many trees. The bacteria trap nitrogen from the air in the soil and convert it into nitrates, which the plant roots can use. The plants repay the bacteria with sugars and other nutrients.

Lichens (LIE-kuhns) are neither plants nor fungi, but intimate partnerships between two or more species of fungi and algae. The algae photosynthesize and provide sugars and proteins, while the fungi take up minerals and prevent the algae from drying out.

## Feeding Partners

Most animals find plant fibers difficult to digest, but many microscopic creatures (microorganisms), including bacteria, produce special chemicals to break them down. Animals that feed mainly on plants take advantage of these microorganisms to

### KEY FACTS

● In the Tropics of the Americas, about 50 different species of birds regularly follow army ants and depend on them for finding food.

● Many plants, from liverworts and ferns to the tallest forest trees, depend on special relationships with fungi, called mycorrhizas, for part of their nutrition.

● A termite just a few millimeters long may have over 100 different kinds of bacteria and other one-celled organisms in its gut that depend on one another.

*Leaf–cutter ants cultivating fungi in their underground nests. The fungi produce fruiting bodies, which the ants feed to their young.*

553

digest their food. Tapirs (TAE-puhrs), deer, rabbits, and other grazing animals have special stomachs or pouches that contain microorganisms to break down the fibers.

Some beetles and termites have an even tougher diet—wood. Their stomachs resemble living zoos, with hundreds of different kinds of microorganisms at work. Without them, termites would starve. The microorganisms are passed on from adults to young when the young termites are fed on a special liquid that the adults produce in their bodies. Ambrosia beetles, found throughout the Tropics, tunnel through tree trunks. They need the help of fungi to rot and soften the wood. They carry their fungi with them from tree to tree in special pockets in the exoskeleton of their head or thorax. Both adults and larvae feed on the fungi that grow in their burrows.

Leaf-cutter ants from Central and South America, as well as some termites, are gardeners—they grow fungi in special underground chambers deep inside their nests. The fungi produce little round fruiting bodies that the ants feed to their young. Some of these fungi are found only in ant nests.

*This sloth's fur is green in color because of the thousands of symbiotic cyanobacteria living there.*

## IN FOCUS

### Honeyguides

In the African forests a bird called a honeyguide has found a novel way of getting into bees' nests to feed on their larvae and wax. When it finds a nest, it seeks out an animal such as a honey badger, or even a human, and leads it to the nest with a strange chattering call, spreading its tail and flying up and down just ahead of it. When the badger or human has broken open the nest and taken the honey, the honeyguide moves in for its own feast.

### Defensive Partnerships

In wet weather, a sloth may appear to have a greenish tinge, blending with the leaves and stems around it. This is due to colorful cyanobacteria that live in grooves in its hairs. In dry weather, the fur reverts to brown, preserving its camouflage. Other creatures make their homes in sloths' fur, too: certain moths and their larvae may take up residence there.

Birds such as oropendolas often build their nests alongside wasp nests. The wasps attack possums or snakes coming to raid the oropendola nests, while the oropendolas drive off caracaras (hawks) that might attack the wasp nest.

## Check these out:

● Ecology ● Ecosystem ● Food Web

# Tapir

Tapirs (TAE-puhrs) are stout-bodied hoofed mammals. Their snouts end in a short, fleshy, trunklike proboscis, (pruh-BAH-sus) which hangs down over their lower lip. This proboscis is really a combined nose and upper lip, with nostrils at its tip. Tapirs are mainly browsers, feeding on green shoots at the edge of forest clearings and along riverbanks. They twist the muscular proboscis around twigs and shoots and pull them off. A large male tapir may be up to 8 feet (2.5 m) long and almost 4 feet (1.2 m) tall and can weigh up to 660 pounds (300 kg). Female tapirs give birth to just one young after a 400-day pregnancy.

There are four species of tapirs: the Brazilian tapir of South America, Baird's tapir in Central and South America, the Malayan tapir of the rain forests of Southeast Asia, and the mountain tapir in the high forests of the Andes. The Malayan tapir has a striking black-and-white coat, which is in fact a good camouflage—it breaks up the animal's outline in the sharply contrasting light and shade in the moonlit forest. The other tapirs are reddish brown with paler bellies. The stripes and spots on the young of all tapir species are also an effective camouflage. They help the young blend in with the dappled sunlight on the forest floor.

## Shy and Secretive

Tapirs live alone and feed mainly at night. They have good hearing and an excellent sense of smell. Shy animals, they live deep in the forest, usually near water or in lush swamps. Except for humans, their only enemies are large predators such as jaguars and tigers. When threatened, they may charge off into the undergrowth; stand and fight, using their teeth as weapons; or plunge into the nearest river and remain almost submerged. They are excellent swimmers.

The biggest threat to tapirs is the loss of their forest habitat. They are also hunted for food, their thick skins, and for sport.

*The stripes of a baby Malayan tapir are in stark contrast to its mother's solid blocks of black and white. Both are well camouflaged in the forest.*

## Check these out:
● Central America  ● Endangered Species  ● Mammal  ● South America

Not all rain forests are hot and humid. In some parts of the world there is enough rainfall to maintain dense forests, even though the climate is temperate, cooler than the Tropics. Today, small areas of these temperate rain forests still survive in the Pacific Northwest of the United States, Alaska, and southwestern Canada, and they grow in small patches high up on the mountains of some Pacific islands. Chile and New Zealand also have temperate evergreen rain forests. There are tiny remnants of them in eastern Asia, but most of the temperate evergreen forests there were felled long ago.

## KEY FACTS

● **Temperate rain forests grow where there is enough rainfall, even though the temperatures are not as high as those in the Tropics.**

● **Approximately 87 percent of the original North American temperate rain forests have already been felled.**

● **The average annual rainfall in the forests of the Pacific Northwest is 145 in. (3,600 mm).**

## Seasons in Temperate Rain Forests

Temperate rain forests, unlike tropical rain forests, have seasons. A mild wet spring is followed by a long, sometimes very dry summer, fading into a wet

*Gaps in the forest, beside lakes or along rivers, support dense mixed vegetation.*

fall, which usually leads to a very hard winter, when the precipitation is still heavy but falls as snow rather than rain. These distinct seasons limit the number of species that can live there. Although the spring and summer flowers produce plenty of fruit in the fall, there is no year-round food supply to maintain hummingbirds and butterflies or leaf-eating animals such as primates. Many butterfly and bird species of the temperate forest migrate to warmer places as winter comes on. Decomposers in temperate rain forests can work only slowly in the cool climate, so any debris from the trees rots down gradually, building up a very rich layer of humus. This provides a home for shade-loving plants such as ferns, which grow in enormous numbers to form a dense, waist-high carpet across the forest floor. At ground level in the temperate forests it is not as dark as in the tropical forests, but it is dark enough for seedlings to find it impossible to grow. Seeds that fall on the forest floor cannot get enough light, so they die as soon as they germinate, unless they fall on a nurse log, a fallen tree that will hold them above the forest floor and in the light.

## North American Fauna and Flora

Temperate rain forests contain fewer species of trees than their tropical counterparts. In North America most of

## A Record Breaker

The tallest tree in the world is a giant redwood, growing in California at the southern edge of the temperate rain forests. More than a thousand years old, it is 367 ft. (111 m) tall.

them are conifers. The principal species there are Douglas fir, red cedar, western hemlock, and Sitka spruce. They are enormous, often growing to more than 300 feet (100 m) tall, and more than 12 feet (3.5 m) across the base. They grow farther apart than trees in tropical forests, and their fine, needlelike leaves carpet the forest floor, making the soil acidic and restricting the ground cover to specialist plants such as ivies and ferns. This makes the interior more spacious than that of a tropical forest. The inside of a temperate rain forest has often been likened to a cathedral, with massive columns soaring high up to the gloomy roof. However, at the edges of the forest, in clearings, and along streams and rivers, there is a huge variety of smaller, broad-leaved trees, shrubs, and flowers.

The ecosystem of these ancient forests depends on the availability of dead wood lying around. As well as helping seedlings to germinate, the rotting logs provide homes and food for a wide variety of ants, beetles, and other insects whose larvae are food for birds such as tree-creepers and woodpeckers. Standing dead trees, known as snags, are dangerous to loggers, because they can fall unpredictably, but they are vital as nesting places for birds and as shelters for animals.

Among the most successful animal species in North American temperate rain forests are a variety of small rodents, such as deer mice and flying squirrels. They in their turn provide food for predators such as the spotted owl, which hunts them in the open spaces among the trees. Larger animals such as elk and black bear haunt the clearings in summer and fall: in winter the elk retreat to forage in the shelter of the forest, and the bears retire to their dens to wait for spring.

## Pacific-Asian Temperate Forests

At one time, extensive evergreen temperate forests flourished in southern China, south Japan, and along the south coast of Korea. They consisted of magnolia and azalea, now valued garden plants all around the world, along with laurels, ginkgo, and stands of bamboo. They once had a rich fauna, including tigers, elephants, and water buffalo, but the forests and the animals are now almost all gone. The tiny fragments that remain are far too small to provide a home for anything larger than some striking butterflies and a few small birds.

The temperate rain forests of the Pacific islands, such as Hawaii, growing high on the mountainsides above the tropical rain forests (which are on the lower slopes), are islands within islands. They grow where the rainfall is heavy enough to support a thick forest but high enough up so that the air is too cool, even close to the equator, to be classed as tropical. These scattered mountain-top areas are very vulnerable because they are so small.

*Black bears can live in temperate rain forests because they can shelter from the winter cold.*

558

# Hawaiian Honeycreepers

On the Hawaiian Islands, the temperate wet forests that grow on the upper slopes of the island of Maui (below) are the last home of a group of birds called honeycreepers. The crested honeycreeper used to live also on Mokolai, but it was wiped out there by introduced predators such as rats and feral cats, which arrived with the first humans about 1,500 years ago. The area where these scarce birds survive is now protected, but it might be too small to support a viable population for very long.

loggers, because their tall, slow-growing trees produce some of the finest—and most valuable—timber in the world. Approximately 87 percent of the original forests have been felled, and another 7 percent is likely to be cut down before all that is left is just over a million acres, already preserved in national parks and other protected areas. These remaining scraps of what was once a huge forest might not be enough to support the wildlife that lives there.

Loggers maintain that by replanting forests to replace trees they have felled, they are creating a sustainable crop that can be harvested again in 10 or 20 years. Conservationists reply that this is not true, because the old forest depends not only on growing trees but on the whole long, slow cycle of death and regeneration, which takes centuries rather than decades to work properly. Tree plantations can never replace the ancient forests—unless they are left alone and untended for two or three hundred years.

**Saving the Temperate Rain Forests**

The North American temperate rain forests are the subject of complicated arguments between conservationists and

## Check these out:
● Bear ● Climate and Weather
● Deforestation ● New Zealand ● North
America ● Season

Termites are social insects. They live in colonies that may contain millions of individuals. Living only in the warmer parts of the world, there are termites in all the tropical rain forests, where they play a major role in recycling dead leaves and twigs.

Although termites look like ants and live in large colonies, they are not ants. While ant colonies are ruled by one or more queens, a termite colony has a king and a queen. Colonies of both insects are populated mainly by workers, but worker ants are all adult females and termite workers are juvenile insects of both sexes. About 5 percent of the termite workforce have very large jaws and are called soldiers. Their job is to defend the colony against ants and other invaders. Although they have no stings, they can inflict deep and painful bites. Worker and soldier termites are all wingless. Only young kings and queens have wings. They swarm out of the nests at certain times of the year, depending on the species, and those that avoid being eaten by birds and other hungry animals pair up and start new colonies.

**KEY FACTS**

● **Although sometimes called white ants, termites are not related to ants.**

● **Some termite queens can lay over 30,000 eggs in a single day. That is over 20 eggs every minute—and they can do this for up to 50 years.**

● **The nests of *Cubitermes* termites have umbrella-like roofs to keep out the rain.**

**Master Builders**

After mating, the queen embarks on a lifetime of egg laying. She can lay several thousand eggs in a day; her body swells up like a sausage as her eggs develop. Some queens can live for 50 years, and a large colony may contain millions of workers. These are all the offspring of the royal pair. The first workers start to build the nest. Many species excavate nests in fallen trees and branches. Other rain forest termites drape their nests over living branches or wrap them around tree trunks. These nests are made with wood that has been chewed up and mixed

*Macrotermes workers use their jaws to cut up a dead stick on the rain forest floor. The pieces will be added to their fungus gardens.*

*What looks like a heap of mud on the rain forest floor is actually a nest. It may hold several thousand termites.*

underground tunnels to reach their food supplies, while others build covered walkways by cementing soil particles together with saliva. Termites are the most numerous creatures in many lowland rain forests, and they play a major role in recycling the dead vegetation. They eat over 10 percent of the leaf litter in the Malaysian rain forest.

The termites themselves cannot digest wood or the tough cellulose of the leaves. Many species carry huge populations of bacteria or other microorganisms inside their bodies, and it is these organisms that break down the food. The termites then absorb some of the digested material. Many other termites, including the mound-building *Macrotermes* species, cultivate fungi (FUN-jie) in their nests. The fungi grow on beds of leaves and twigs brought in by the termites, and the termites then eat the fungi.

with saliva and the termites' droppings. Some termites excavate subterranean nests, while others build huge mounds by excavating soil and cementing the particles together with saliva and droppings. When dry, the walls are as hard as concrete. These huge nests are equipped with air-conditioning systems and ventilation chimneys. The biggest ones, up to 20 feet (6 m) high, are on the African savannas, but there are some large nests in the rain forests as well. Most of these belong to the *Macrotermes* species.

## Vegetarian Diets

The termite king and queen live in a royal chamber near the center of the nest. They are constantly fed and tended by the workers. Unlike ants, termites are all vegetarians. They feed on living and dead leaves and seeds, and dead wood. The wood-feeding species can do enormous damage to houses.

Termites do not venture into the open very much. Many species move through

## IN FOCUS

# Chemical Warfare

Some termites produce a strange kind of soldier whose head forms a nozzle. These termite soldiers, called nasutes, squirt sticky fluid at their enemies. The fluid hardens quickly and immobilizes the invader. Some nasute species produce poisonous fluids.

## Check these out:
- **Bacteria**  - **Feeding**  - Herbivore  - Insect
- **Nest and Nest Building**  - **Symbiosis**

# Tiger

The tiger is the top predator in the jungles of Southeast Asia, from the rain forests of Indonesia to the vast swamps of the Sundarbans in Bangladesh. Standing over 3 feet (1 m) tall at the shoulder, and stretching up to 6½ feet (2.2 m) long, with a tail about half that length, a male tiger is a formidable animal.

The tigers of Southeast Asia are a bright reddish tan, with striking near black stripes. The stripes help to break up the tiger's outline as it moves stealthily through the forest. The underparts are white. There is a large white spot over each eye and often another on the back of each ear. Tigers that live in the cooler climates farther north are paler.

Tigers do most of their hunting at night. A powerful animal, the tiger can kill prey as large as deer and even buffalo, cattle, and elephants. It usually attacks old or sick animals, and it also hunts smaller prey, such as jungle fowl and wild pigs. A tiger hunts by stalking its prey very quietly until it is close enough to pounce.

## KEY FACTS

● **All subspecies of tigers are endangered, and some are already extinct.**

● **There may only be about 5,000 tigers left in the wild today.**

● **Tigers can be bred with lions. If the father is a tiger, the offspring is called a tigon. If the mother is a tiger, the offspring is a liger.**

## Breeding

In the Tropics, tigers may breed all year round. They communicate by both scent and sound. Males will roar loudly in the mating season—this carries their message through the dense forest. Females usually produce two or three cubs, which stay with their mother for over a year. Like the young of most big cats, they have to learn to hunt and kill before they can become independent.

*A five-month-old Indian tiger cub nuzzles up to its mother. It will stay with her for over a year until it has learned to hunt for itself.*

*A rare Sumatran tiger shakes water from its body after plunging through a river. Rapid deforestation threatens to make this subspecies extinct soon.*

The mother tiger will not breed again until her cubs have left, and she will live for only about 11 years. Where tiger numbers are reduced by hunting or loss of habitat, it is hard for them to recover with such a slow rate of breeding.

**Vanishing Tigers**

There are several tiger subspecies, including the Indian tiger (the most common in Southeast Asia), the Sumatran tiger, and the Siberian tiger. They are all endangered. The Javan, Bali, and Caspian tigers are already extinct, and the Chinese tiger is almost extinct.

At the beginning of the 20th century, there were about 100,000 wild tigers. Today there may be only as few as 5,000. In the first part of the 20th century, tigers were hunted mainly for sport—as trophies (heads to hang on walls or skins to use as rugs), and for expensive fur coats.

In the 1970s most countries introduced bans on the shooting of tigers and on trading in skins, but tigers are also killed for their body parts, which are used in Chinese medicines. Tiger parts are said to cure rheumatism and other diseases and to act as aphrodisiacs (love potions). The rarer the tiger gets, the higher the price paid for its skin and body parts, and the greater the temptation to kill tigers.

Another serious threat is the loss of the tiger's forest home as human populations increase and cut down forest to create farmland. Deprived of both food and shelter, the tiger is attracted to populated areas, often killing cattle, whereupon it is likely to be shot.

## Man-Eaters

**IN FOCUS**

From time to time tigers take to killing people, but humans are not their normal prey. Man-eaters are usually old or disabled tigers that have difficulty catching more agile animals. Once a tiger has begun to kill people, it usually continues, so there is no choice but to shoot it.

## Check these out:

- Asia
- Carnivore
- Cat
- Endangered Species
- Food Web
- Mammal

# Tlingit People

The Tlingit (TLING-ket) are a native people of the temperate rain forest of the North American Pacific Coast. They live along the southeastern coast of Alaska and the coast of British Columbia. Some Tlingits also live inland in those areas, extending into Yukon Territory. In the 1990s their population was about 17,000.

Historically, the Tlingits have been organized into more than a dozen local groups. Each group had its own area, which might consist of up to six villages. These groups spoke different dialects, and there were also differences in customs.

## Western Influences

Many Tlingits began being lured away from their traditional life during the Klondike gold rush in the 1890s. Today, Tlingits are

### KEY FACTS

● There are about 17,000 Tlingits; they live in the temperate rain forest of the North American Pacific Coast.

● In 1971 the Alaska Native Claims Settlement Act created the Sealaska Corporation and gave the Tlingit self-determination.

● Tlingits hold potlatch ceremonies where a host gives away many of his possessions to his guests.

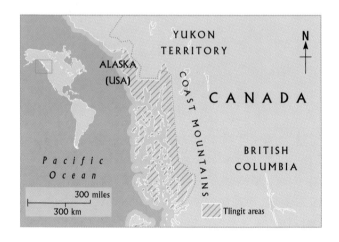

integrated into the economy of Alaska. Many Tlingits have jobs in the lumber and fisheries industries.

Tlingits and other native people of Alaska have worked hard to maintain their rights as indigenous peoples. In 1971 their efforts were rewarded with the passage of the Alaska Native Claims Settlement Act.

Under the act, 13 native corporations are now in operation, with the native people being shareholders in their corporations. The Tlingits are joined with their neighbors, the Haida people, in the Sealaska Corporation, which manages their tribal resources. The act assures that native people will have a future in Alaska.

*A Tlingit elder in ceremonial dress.*

## Potlatch

A potlatch is a great feast that lasts for days. During the potlatch the hosts give away their wealth to their guests, thereby increasing their status. The more goods they give away, the greater the stature they obtain. Some potlatches require years of planning. They are observed with formality, according to ancient traditions, and are memorial ceremonies for the dead. Potlatches were less frequent during the 1950s and 1960s as many Tlingits focused on adapting to the American economy, but a revival of pride in Tlingit traditional life assured their continuation.

### Living with the Rain Forest

The abundance of the rain forest provided Tlingits with lumber for large wooden buildings that housed up to a dozen families. Today most Tlingits live in separate houses in nuclear families. Tlingit craftsmen developed an art of converting rain forest trees into intricately carved totem poles honoring Tlingit ancestors. This art is being revived today.

Traditional healers among the Tlingits possess a store of knowledge of the medical uses of rain

forest plants. This knowledge has been acquired through many centuries of intimate acquaintance with their rain forest environment.

In Tlingit culture, the stories, songs, designs, house crests, and other artistic and intellectual property are owned by individual people and can be passed down by inheritance. These things continue to have great importance for Tlingit people.

Today, most Tlingits still live in coastal towns in the historical locations of their villages. Their lives have been changed greatly by the arrival of American industry, especially logging and commercial fisheries. Traditional Tlingit economic life has largely been replaced by the new economy, but Tlingit ceremonial life continues to endure.

### Check these out:

● North America ● People of the Rain Forest ● Temperate Rain Forest

*Tlingits are known for their skill in carving wood for totem poles, as seen on this traditional Tlingit house.*

# Toucan

Toucans are medium- to large-sized birds of the Central and South American Tropics, famous for their huge bills, which may make up a third of their body length. The deep, flattened bill is often very brightly colored, sometimes with distinct patterns. Many toucans also have bright patches of bare skin around their eyes, as well as showy breast colors. They have long tails for steering, and short, rounded wings ideal for flying in dense forest.

Toucans are up to 2 feet (60 cm) long, depending on the species, and have mainly black bodies with splashes of color. Their smaller relatives are the slender aracaris and the greenish toucanets.

## KEY FACTS

● Toucans often bathe in the pools of water that collect in hollow branches high in the canopy.

● When sleeping, a toucan lays its bill along its back, then cocks its tail back over its head to cover its bill.

● There are about 40 species of toucans, including 12 species of toucanets and 11 species of aracaris.

Noisy birds, toucans live in groups of about 12 and roost high in the treetops. They nest in holes in tree trunks, usually formed naturally as the wood decays. The toucan's large bill is not adapted for drilling holes, but it can enlarge them by removing rotting wood. Toucan nest holes have a small entrance but may be over 6 feet (2 m) deep.

*The keel–billed toucan from Central America is often nicknamed the banana bill. The bird's huge bill is used for feeding, grooming, signaling, and fighting.*

*A groove-billed toucanet from Venezuela surveys the forest. Small toucans are often called toucanets.*

## Toucan Play

Toucans use their bills for what appears to be a kind of play. They sometimes clack bills together or toss fruits to each other using their bills. They also wrestle, grasping each other's bills and pushing and twisting until one gives up.

### Multipurpose Bill

Toucans feed on fruit, large insects, baby birds, and lizards. The huge bill has sawlike edges, perhaps to help grip fruit. The toucan picks up the fruit with the tip of its bill, then tosses back its head and juggles the fruit in its bill until it can throw it into its throat. The long bill also acts like an arm—the toucan can reach fruits some distance away, even on twigs that would not support the bird's weight. The bill is not heavy—it is supported by many fine, criss-crossing fibers inside, with hollows in between.

Toucans use their bills to defend themselves and also for the delicate task of grooming each other: a bill that can pluck a small berry from a twig can also extract tiny parasites from other birds' feathers.

The showy colors of toucan bills—and of toucans themselves—may act as flags to indicate who is who. Each individual bird's bill is a slightly different size and has different patterns of colors. It may indicate to other toucans the species to which the bird belongs, important when competing for mates or nest holes. The color may also startle other birds so that they leave their nests, allowing the toucan to help itself to their eggs or young.

### Growing Up

Toucans lay their eggs on a carpet of wood chips deep inside a tree hole. They lay two to four shiny white eggs, and the male and female take turns incubating them. When they hatch, the chicks are blind and have no feathers. Their eyes open after about three weeks, but their feathers take up to seven weeks to grow. Until then, the chicks stay in the nest hole and are fed by their parents. At first their bills are small and dull, but as the young toucans grow, their bills get bigger and become brightly colored.

Young toucans have rough pads on their heels; they rest on these while in the nest. The pads may protect their feet from the hard wood chips and seed husks that cover the floor of the nest.

## Check these out:
● Bird  ● South America

The first explorers of the rain forests would have found it hard to imagine that in the late 20th and early 21st centuries rain forests would be a popular tourist destination. The Sanskrit word *jangala* is used by Indian people to mean simply "desert" or "wasteland," but it soon came to have darker overtones when it was adopted into English. To the early explorers, jungles were threatening and inhospitable places, filled with dangerous snakes and insects that carried disease, not to mention terrifying large apes and poisonous vines.

Today, though, the surviving rain forests attract visitors from all over the world, keen to see for themselves the wonderful sights they have seen on television. This form of vacation is sometimes called ecotourism. The people who do it travel not to admire buildings or experience foreign cultures, nor to bask on coral beaches in permanent sunshine, but specifically to see wildlife in unspoiled surroundings. For some small countries, such as Costa Rica (which had one million visitors to its 28 parks and reserves in 2000), it is a major source of income.

Tourism not only brings in foreign currency for the country, but it also provides jobs for local people, especially members of forest-living groups, who

**KEY FACTS**

● **Tourism can be an important source of income for rain forest people.**

● **Tourists can act as witnesses for the rest of the world, encouraging people to look after the rain forest.**

● **In 2000, one million people visited Costa Rica's 28 parks and reserves.**

*The trip of a lifetime: tourists view the rain forests of Thailand from elephant-back.*

*Specially built resorts make life comfortable for tourists. This camp is in the central plaza of a Maya ruin in Belize.*

harm the forest. At its most obvious, this means not creating litter or starting fires, but there are other important considerations. Streams of people crashing through the forest can disturb the animals that live there and can compact the delicate forest soil. The answer is to sacrifice part of the forest so as to protect the rest. This means cutting clear paths through the forest, along which people can walk without disturbing the vegetation on either side. Animals quickly become used to people passing, when they realize that they mean them no harm. Sometimes cutting is unnecessary, because the people who live in the forest already have their own paths, which might have been used for hundreds of years.

know more about their forest home than scientists from overseas will ever discover. In undeveloped areas such as Irian Jaya, in Indonesia, it can be the only way in which local people can be encouraged to preserve the forests as a source of income. A new campground and resort beside Kenyir Lake, on the edge of a large rain forest reserve, is among the latest developments in Indonesia designed to encourage ecotourism.

Another important function of ecotourists is as witnesses who can carry back to the rest of the world reports on how the environment is being managed in these remote places. Maintaining beautiful areas of forest with populations of rare plants and animals may seem like an end in itself to enthusiasts in developed countries, but to the people who live in rain forest areas and depend on them for their survival, tourism is the main motivation for conserving their environment.

**Protecting Forests from Tourists**

However, it is not enough just to guide people into the forest and explain what they can see. Care must be taken to ensure that the activities of visitors do not

## Alaskan Forests

**IN FOCUS**

In the temperate rain forests beside Prince William Sound, in Alaska, there are other constraints on tourists. There, the locals prefer small groups of visitors, backpackers rather than large guided parties. This is partly to avoid disturbance, but also because the local Eyak Indians have several sacred sites in the forests beside the sea, which must be treated with respect.

## Check these out:
- Careers ● Exploitation ● Forestry
- Human Interference ● National Park

# Tree

A tree is a long-lived woody plant that produces new growth every year. It has a single main stalk for support—the trunk—which distinguishes trees from shrubs. The main trunk is usually at least 15 feet (4.5 m) tall when mature, although in harsh environments many plants are considered to be trees even though they do not reach this height. Shrubs usually branch much closer to the ground than trees. However, the same species may form trees in some habitats and shrubs in others. Many different kinds of plants are trees, including flowering trees, conifers, cycads, and tree ferns.

## Forest Architects

Trees shape the rain forest. There are often many layers of trees at different heights. The crowns of the big forest trees form the canopy, a green roof that shades the forest below and keeps it warm and moist. The canopy is home to

*A flooded forest, or **igapo**, fringes the Negro River in Brazil, a tributary of the Amazon. These trees may be inundated for several months. The green carpet is of water weeds, not grass.*

many different kinds of animals, from monkeys to mice, which feed on its leaves, flowers, and fruits and use it as a safe route across the forest, out of reach of predators on the forest floor. Birds and squirrels build their nests among the branches, and ants and termites make their paper homes on trunks and branches, attracting predators such as anteaters and pangolins.

Many other plants grow on the branches and tree trunks of these forest giants. Even the leaves may become covered in tiny gardens of mosses and lichens. Orchids, bromeliads (broe-MEE-lee-ads), and ferns often have dense tufts of leaves and tangled roots that provide shelter for many invertebrates and small frogs, salamanders, lizards, and snakes. When old trees become rotten and hollow, quetzals (ket-SAHLS), hornbills, woodpeckers, parrots, macaws, and many other birds can nest in them, as well as mammals like raccoons. More animals live among the dense tangle of understory trees, shrubs, and lianas (lee-AH-nuhs), including many that forage on the forest floor but need to escape to safer places to feed and sleep.

Armies of roots reach out through the soil, trapping moisture from the heavy

# Eucalypts

Eucalyptus trees are common in subtropical Australian rain forest. They include some of the tallest trees in the world. They litter the forest floor with strips of peeled bark. Constant peeling prevents epiphytes, climbers, and fungi from getting a hold on the bark. Eucalyptus trunks are often streaked with bare blue or gray new bark. Some, such as the ghost gum of northern Australia, are gleaming white. When it rains, resin from the trunk streams down in the runoff in a bubbly stream, helping to wash the trunk clean. Eucalypts also readily shed their branches if damaged, leaving holes that provide shelters and nest sites for many birds, mammals, and reptiles. The droppings from these animals supply the tree with extra nutrients.

tropical rain and keeping it in the forest, rather than letting it run away into rivers. The folds between the huge roots provide hollows that serve as dens for foxes, cats, and other predators on the forest floor, as well as for smaller creatures such as mice. Even the leaf litter on the forest floor supports a teeming world of millipedes, centipedes, spiders, beetles, worms, snails, and many other small invertebrates.

## Reaching for the Light

Forests are dominated by trees, but why are trees so successful? Growing tall enables a plant to reach above other plants and get more light for photosynthesis. It can use the wind for pollination and spore or seed dispersal, and its very height means that seeds shed from its upper branches will travel a long way on the wind.

The large crown of branches has thousands of leaves to absorb sunlight and produce food for growth. They feed a large network of branches, the trunk, and the roots. The roots anchor the tree and ensure a good supply of water and minerals for the tree—and less for its neighbors.

However, in growing and maintaining such a large body, the plant uses a lot of energy. A tree has to grow a thicker trunk as it grows taller in order to support the increasing weight. More cells need more food from the roots and leaves. Trees have evolved a neat solution to this problem: most of the trunk of a large forest tree is made up of dead tissue—the wood. This tissue provides support but does not need feeding.

The roots, which have to supply all the water and minerals for the tree, have hidden helpers. Most rain forest trees form close partnerships with certain fungi, (FUN-jie) called mycorrhizas, which help them to extract minerals from the soil. While the fungi provide the trees with extra nutrients, the trees pass on to the fungi the sugars they have made through photosynthesis; thus both partners benefit.

## The Shapes of Trees

Rain forest trees range from small understory specimens that often have rather tall, narrow crowns to the giant trees of the main forest canopy with their great spreading crowns and the even taller emergents that grow out into the sunlight above the canopy. Some of these emergents, such as the Southeast Asian tualang, may be 270 feet (85 m) tall.

The shape of a tree is due partly to its genetic makeup and partly to the stresses it encounters from its environment while it is growing. Factors such as light, wind, and soil nutrients affect the tree's growth. If the young tree has to compete for light with its neighbors, it will grow taller and narrower than if it is out in the open by itself. Many canopy and emergent trees, such as *Shorea*, found in Southeast Asia, have narrow, pointed crowns when young, but spread out once they reach the sunlight. In a windy spot a tree may

**IN FOCUS**

## Losing Leaves

A typical leaf lives for 3 to 15 months, then it dies and drops off and new leaves unfurl. Most rain forest trees are always shedding a few leaves, so they never appear bare, but some shed them all at once. The silk cotton tree, for example, sheds its leaves just before the flower buds open, so the crown becomes a mass of flowers uninterrupted by leaves. This helps its bird pollinators to spot it. Tropical trees often produce lots of new leaves at once, so only a few will be lost to herbivores.

*Giant buttresses support the towering trunk of an emergent in the montane rain forest of Pahang, in West Malaysia. Climbing plants take advantage of the moisture and shade between buttresses.*

gets wider and the tree develops a large, dead, but very strong core.

A few of the larger trees produce buttress roots— large, flattened winglike roots that grow out from the trunk well above the ground and form flanges around the trunk. The hollows between these roots provide shelter for a host of small animals and a moist, shady habitat for ferns.

### Far-Flung Young

In the subtropics, trees may flower in particular seasons, but there are no true seasons in the Tropics, and individuals of the same species may be found flowering all year round. However, some trees, such as the dipterocarps of Southeast Asia, all flower at once, creating vast areas of color. They then set fruit at the same time, satiating the animals that would eat both fruit and seeds, so improving the chances of seed dispersal.

Like other plants, trees produce spores or seeds that will grow into the next generation. The shade of a big canopy tree is not the ideal place for its seeds to germinate, so trees need to have their seeds dispersed. Tree ferns produce spores, while cycads, conifers, and flowering plants produce seeds. In the still air below the canopy, only a few

produce more branches downwind, or it may be stunted. If nutrients are in short supply, this, too, can stunt a tree's growth.

### Tremendous Trunks

Tall trees need a lot of support, which is supplied by a strong substance called lignin. Lignin is found in the walls of the xylem vessels. These are tubelike cells that run up the trunk, carrying water from the roots to the leaves.

With time, the xylem vessels become blocked with air or debris, so the tree produces a new ring of xylem on the outside of the old xylem. Thus the trunk plants with extremely light silky seeds or winged fruits rely on air currents. Some produce vast clouds of feather-light fluffy seeds that float through the forest and settle like drifts of cotton wool on the forest floor.

Animals are often used to carry seeds away. Such seeds lie inside juicy fruits with attractive red or orange coats. Animals eat the flesh of the fruit, and the seeds pass right through them and are deposited with their droppings.

Most rain forest trees produce large seeds with good food stores. These provide the energy for seedlings to grow tall enough to reach the light and start photosynthesis. The food stores also

*A flowering dipterocarp in the rain forest of Thailand. The tree sheds many of its leaves just before flowering, so the flowers can be seen by pollinators from a considerable distance.*

attract animals, for whom seedlings provide a tender, nutritious meal. Some trees, such as the Southeast Asian dipterocarps, produce masses of seeds that all germinate together, swamping animals that would eat them and crowding out competing seedlings.

## Getting Started
Rain forest trees have two main strategies for competing. Some produce seedlings that can survive for a long time without growing very big. They lie in wait, ready to take advantage of light if the area around them becomes exposed when a large tree is felled or is knocked down by a storm. Others produce seeds that lie dormant in the soil. These seeds will not germinate until the light from above is strong enough, indicating that a clearing, or light gap, has formed. All these seedlings have to grow quickly to outcompete each other.

The fastest-growing trees are the first to fill the gap in the canopy; many of them live for around 100 years. But in time, slow-growing, shade-tolerant trees will grow up and replace them, and these trees may live for 200 to 500 years or even longer. This succession of trees adds to the great diversity of species in the rain forest. With them come all the animals and epiphytes adapted to live on and around the different tree species.

## Exploiting Trees
Rain forests are sources of food and medicines for local people, and they also attract outsiders who come for timber or seek

other products such as dyes, rubber, and gums. There is increasing exploration of forests to find new kinds of drugs.

Rain forest trees are the sources of peppers; fruits such as avocado, mango, and papaya; spices such as mace and nutmeg, allspice, cinnamon, and cloves; and oils such as ylang-ylang, rosewood, sandalwood, and eucalyptus.

Many important timbers come from the rain forest. Some are now grown in plantations, but others, such as mahogany, are difficult to cultivate and in any case take around a hundred years to mature. These are often taken from the rain forest. Felling such large trees brings down many others, and the roads built by logging companies to remove the timber provide a route for settlers from the cities, who burn and fell the forest to make small, often unsustainable farms.

Among the valuable timbers from the rain forest are ebony, sapele (used for furniture, plywood, and doors), and mahogany from Africa; balsa (a very light wood used for making model airplanes), greenheart (a heavy, durable timber used in industrial flooring and in docks and harbors, as it resists marine-boring animals), and mahogany from the Americas; and teak from Southeast Asia. Mangroves are used for making particleboard, leaving some tropical coasts at risk from flooding where they are cleared indiscriminately.

Among the many pharmaceuticals extracted from rain forest trees are poisons

such as strychnine, medicines such as the antimalarial drug quinine, and insecticides such as *quassia*.

## Check these out:

- Canopy
- Dormancy
- Emergent
- Flowering Plant
- Leaf
- Light Gap
- Logging
- Plant
- Rain Forest
- Root
- Seed
- Understory

IN FOCUS

# Tree Ferns

Tree ferns are large ferns with treelike trunks that look like palms. The leaves surround the trunk, and as the fern grows taller, the lowermost leaves die, leaving woody leaf bases that wrap around the trunk. Much of the trunk's width is made up of leaf bases, which also provide platforms for epiphytes such as orchids and other ferns. In some mountain forests, shrouded in mist and cloud, very tall tree ferns may emerge above the forest canopy.

575

Tree frogs live in the Tropics and subtropics all over the world except in Australia. They are found throughout the rain forest, from the lowest leaves to the top of the canopy, where some live around the tiny pools that form in the center of epiphytes such as bromeliads (broe-MEE-lee-ads). Some feed on small invertebrates, while larger species may take small lizards or other frogs. Tree frogs come in a rainbow of colors—from green and yellow to pink, blue, and violet.

Small, light frogs, they cling to the leaves with suction-cup fingers and toes. Tree frogs from the Americas also have loose skin on their bellies to help them stick to foliage. Their bodies are much flatter than those of other frogs, which makes it easier for them to balance and travel from leaf to leaf. On most continents there are certain tree frogs that have developed very large webs between their toes, which enable them to glide from tree to tree—much safer than traveling over the ground.

## Camouflage and Other Defenses

Small frogs are constantly at risk of attack from birds, so they have developed a number of defenses. Leaf frogs are green and come out mostly at night. Some leaf frogs have striking bright red eyes to startle attackers. Many leaf frogs have brilliant flashes of black and yellow or orange on the insides of their thighs. When threatened, they flash these colors to startle the attacker.

The little green glass frogs of Central and South America have almost transparent skin, with their hearts and most of their other internal organs clearly visible. They rest by pressing themselves against leaves. The color of the leaf

*A poison dart frog is calling to declare his ownership of a territory. The inflated throat sac acts like a resonator to amplify his calls, while his bright colors warn that he is poisonous.*

## IN FOCUS

### Frog Choruses

Frogs use calling to attract mates. They gather at favorite breeding pools and start to call. As the chorus gets louder, frogs farther and farther away hear it and converge on the pool. Tree frogs have inflatable throat sacs that help them make quite loud noises. The reed frogs of Africa have huge throat sacs, almost as big as the rest of their bodies when inflated.

shows through their bodies and makes them hard to spot.

Poison dart frogs, have the opposite strategy. Their skin contains lethal poisons, which they advertise with brilliant colors—black and yellow, orange, red, and even blue and yellow—in some amazing patterns. Their defense does not depend on concealment, so they are active by day, hunting among the leaves on the forest floor or in the undergrowth.

**Eggs in Strange Places**

There are many tiny pools in which tree frogs can lay their eggs—in bromeliads and other rosette epiphytes, in between the overlapping fronds of ferns, or in hollows in old tree trunks. There are also small pools on the forest floor.

Many tree frogs lay their eggs on leaves. Leaf frogs and glass frogs lay their eggs on leaves overhanging water. The male glass frog guards his eggs until they hatch, after which the tadpoles drop straight into the water.

Many tree frogs, especially those from South and Central America and Africa,

*Two glass frogs guard their eggs in the rain forest of Costa Rica. Their transparent bodies are hard to spot. Tiny tadpoles are already developing inside the eggs.*

make foam nests into which they shed their eggs and sperm. The frogs produce a fluid that they kick into a foam. The foam hardens like a meringue and sticks the eggs to a leaf while they develop.

A few tree frogs have altogether done away with the need for water. The marsupial frogs of Central and South America carry their eggs in watery depressions in the skin on the back of the female. The eggs hatch into tadpoles and then develop into tiny frogs. The mother claws at the skin to free them, and they hop away.

Poison dart frogs lay their eggs on the ground and guard them until the tadpoles hatch. The tadpoles wriggle, one at a time, onto the back of one of their parents and are carried to a bromeliad pool. The female returns from time to time to feed the tadpoles with an infertile egg.

## Check these out:

● Amphibian ● Courtship ● Frog and Toad

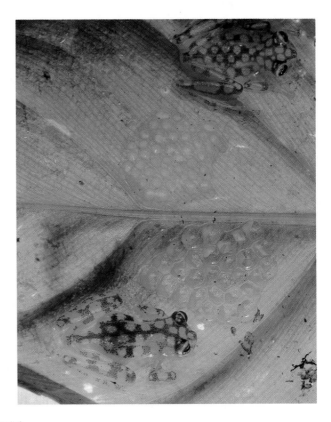

# Tree Kangaroo

Tree kangaroos live in the more remote and inaccessible areas of the rain forests of Queensland, Australia, and New Guinea. Like other ground-dwelling kangaroos and wallabies, tree kangaroos are marsupials and rear their babies in a pouch. As their name implies, tree kangaroos spend their lives up in the rain forest canopy. They are roughly the size of the more familiar wallabies but tend to be more thick-set with shorter, broader muzzles. The overall body length of the seven recognized species lies between 20 and 32 inches (52 and 81 cm), plus a tail 17 to 36 inches (42 to 92 cm) long. Though they live in trees, the furry tail is not prehensile like that of some monkeys. It is used instead for balancing.

Tree kangaroo fur is fairly long, silky in some species and rough in others, and may be strikingly marked. Goodfellow's tree kangaroo, for example, has reddish fur on the back with yellow lines along each side of the spine. The underside, hands, feet, and face are bright yellow, while the tail is mottled, brown and yellow.

## Climbing and Walking

Tree kangaroos are not very often seen because they live high in the trees and are active at night. To help them move around in the trees, they have big feet with rough-skinned pads, like cushions. These rough pads prevent the feet from slipping on the bark of the tree; a number of their claws are curved to improve their grip.

Quite agile, these animals can move quickly through the trees, jumping down as much as 30 feet (9 m) as they move from one tree to another. They have even been seen to jump 60 feet (18 m) from a tree down to the

*A tree kangaroo in Australia, glimpsed during the day. These animals are nocturnal and seldom seen, even by local people.*

*A black tree kangaroo climbs a tree in the New Guinea forest, aided by its very long claws.*

ground without apparent injury. Normally, however, they come down to the ground more gently, by walking backward down the trunk of the tree, holding it tightly with the rough pads and claws on their feet. Once on the ground they walk or take small jumps rather than hop like the ground-dwelling kangaroos and wallabies. It is quite probable that tree kangaroos were once ground dwellers but moved up into the trees to escape from predators.

Tree kangaroos emerge at dusk to find their food, which consists of leaves, fruit, and tree bark. The black tree kangaroo of New Guinea has also been seen to eat ferns and creepers. Having spent the night foraging they then retire to sleep at dawn. Some species spend the day sleeping alone or in small mixed groups but the Doria tree kangaroo from New Guinea is unusual. The dominant male lives with a small group of females. One offspring is produced at a time, and like other kangaroos, it remains in the mother's pouch until it is old enough to leave.

While all species of tree kangaroo are threatened by the loss of their habitat, those from New Guinea face an extra threat: they are eaten by local people.

## Check these out:

● **Australia** ● **Indonesia** ● **Mammal**
● **Nocturnal Animal**

### IN FOCUS

## Keeping Dry

The thick fur on the tree kangaroo's nape (back of the neck) is unusual in that it grows forward, in the opposite direction to that of the rest of the fur. Tree kangaroos sit head-down when it is raining, and the forward-growing fur helps to shed the water from the back of the head and neck.

579

An exact definition of what constitutes a tropical rain forest is hard to come by, especially since one type of forest may gradually merge into another with changes in altitude or soils. However, certain conditions are specific to tropical rain forests.

Tropical lowland rain forest is always more or less evergreen, a state that is brought about by the almost constant supply of water and heat. Rainfall varies somewhat but is never less than about 80 inches (2,000 mm) per year. Just as important as the amount of rainfall is the fact that it arrives more or less consistently throughout the year, with no prolonged dry period, and at least some rain falls even in the driest months. Temperature is also vital. It must

## KEY FACTS

● **More than three-quarters of all the terrestrial animal species on Earth come from tropical rain forests.**

● **Rainfall in some tropical rain forests can reach 325 in. (8,200 mm) per year.**

● **Tropical rain forest now covers only about 5 percent of Earth's land surface.**

● **The fig is the most important source of food for fruit-eating rain forest animals.**

*The rain forest generates much of its own rainfall, visible as white clouds that form just above the forest canopy.*

average at least 75°F (24°C), with no frosts. This combination of constant humidity and pervading warmth gives rise to a typical forest of very tall trees, many of which have buttress roots fanning out from the base. In most tropical rain forests the trees are abundantly draped with riotous tangles of lianas (lee-AH-nuhs) and epiphytic plants such as ferns, aroids, orchids, bromeliads (broe-MEE-lee-ads), and cacti.

Tropical rain forest once flourished over a broad band of the equatorial belt between the tropic of Cancer in the north and the tropic of Capricorn in the south. Since 1900 this forest area has been slashed in half by human activities, and the rate of destruction has significantly increased since the 1980s. The main areas of tropical rain forest today are in South America and Southeast Asia (mainly Indonesia), with smaller areas in south Asia (India and Sri Lanka). In Africa the giant Ituri rain forest covers large areas of the Congo River basin, but rain forest also occurs widely in West Africa, in Guinea, the Ivory Coast, and Cameroon. Madagascar, Central America, the West Indies, Australia, New Guinea, and some of the Pacific islands have smaller but important areas of rain forest. Today the largest continuous area of tropical rain forest lies in the Amazon basin, much of which is still an unexplored wilderness pierced by numerous rivers and home to thousands

# Rain Forest Mimics

You can never be quite sure what you are looking at in a rain forest. Ants are everywhere, but they are not always what they seem. A closer look may reveal that some of them are really spiders, imposters that look and behave so much like ants that only an expert can tell them apart. Spiders have eight legs and no antennae, while ants have six legs and two antennae. Spiders that mimic ants use their pair of front legs as realistic substitutes, waving them around just like real antennae. Wasps, also common in rain forests, are mimicked by a whole range of other insects, including bugs, moths, spiders, and crane flies (below).

of species of plants and animals, many of which have yet to be discovered.

## A Delicately Balanced Environment

Many years ago colonists from European countries looking at the luxuriant growth of the rain forest, with its mighty trees and mass of exuberant greenery, dreamed of how all this land could be turned into farms on which the production of milk, meat, and crops would exceed anything hitherto known. This vision was based on the assumption that to produce such a

*Relatively little light filters down to the rain forest understory, which is often full of climbers and other shade–tolerant plants.*

is immediately reused by the roots of the trees, which in tropical rain forests are very shallow. They spread out wide around the base of the tree, rather than going down deep, as happens in temperate forests with their rich, deep soils. These shallow roots mean that rain forest trees are easily felled by winds and storms, although the buttresses that have evolved on so many kinds are some form of protection. Decay in the forest is so rapid under the constant heat and rain that there is no buildup of the dense carpet of dead leaves found in most temperate forests. The rain forest exists by consuming its own waste in a highly efficient manner that permits virtually no escape of nutrients from the ecosystem.

luxuriant forest, the soils must be among the richest on Earth and that the rain would never fail. We now know that both these assumptions are false.

Many rain forest soils are in fact very poor and thin, and the forest exists only because it constantly recycles its own nutrients. The leaves falling from above are rapidly decomposed by fungi (FUN-jie) and bacteria, aided by the actions of insects such as termites. Even massive fallen tree trunks are eventually broken down to their constituent chemicals by the persistent action of fungal decomposers. The resulting humus

The other vital factor in the forest is rainfall, which is also generated by the forest. As the millions of huge trees shunt a constant supply of evaporated water out from their leaves and up into the already humid atmosphere, it quickly condenses to form clouds. This system is so efficient that three-quarters of the water released by the forest is quickly returned to it as rain.

## IN FOCUS

# Leaves

Many young leaves are bright red, then change to green as they develop. In the canopy this red coloration protects the tender young leaves against the harsh sunlight. The chemical that gives the red tint also forms the basis for defensive compounds. Rain forest leaves suffer because they are so long-lived (they may last for over a year, compared with just a single season for leaves in most temperate species). Encouraged by the humid atmosphere, the leaves may soon be covered with a coating of mosses and other epiphytic plants called epiphylls. Many rain forest leaves have drip tips that help shed the water quickly, hindering the establishment of epiphylls.

If the cycle is broken by felling, the rain is lost, and this has already happened in many parts of the world where deforestation has been extensive.

## Animals and Plants

On a safari in the great savanna grasslands of Africa, a tourist could see thousands of large animals in just a single day. Yet after walking through any rain forest for a few hours, he or she may wonder where all the animals are. Tropical rain forests have by far the highest biodoversity of any habitat, with millions of species. So why can't they be seen? One reason is that most of the rain forest's animals are insects, and most of these are up out of sight in the sunlit canopy. The largest animals living today in rain forests are elephants and rhinos (in Africa and Asia), but these occur in very low numbers. The biggest animals now found in the forests of Central and South America are tapirs (TAE-puhrs), which are smaller than the average cow, are solitary, and live scattered over a large area. The fact is that the rain forest offers a poor larder for the average large grazing animal because much of the vegetation contains defensive chemicals. Consequently, many rain forest animals, such as rhinos, just take a bite here and a bite there, avoiding the kind of harmful buildup of toxins that would result from feeding exclusively on a single type of plant.

Other rain forest plants protect their leaves with tough waxy coatings or with a battery of stinging hairs, such as the stinging nettle tree in Australia, whose sting can kill a human if enough skin comes into contact with the leaves and stems. Many leaves contain bitter-tasting tannins, which deter animals from taking

# Protecting Young

Insects face many kinds of enemies in the rain forest, especially ants, which occur in millions from the forest floor to the high canopy and are voracious predators. The larval stages of insects are especially at risk, so it is not surprising that in some species the females stay behind to guard their eggs and young, rather than abandoning them. Parental care is quite common in stinkbugs and treehoppers, but less so in beetles, so the three species of South American tortoise beetles that protect their offspring from egg to adult are especially interesting. The females will valiantly drive away small enemies such as ants and assassin bugs that threaten their young.

group of enemies—the insects—which eat the poisonous leaves without harm and then use the poisons as their own defense.

**Feeding the Forest**

The rain forest canopy is a thoroughfare for a great deal of animal life such as monkeys and birds that are difficult to see from the ground. Many of these animals feed on fruits, of which a good proportion are packed with defensive chemicals, designed to make the fruits unattractive until they are ripe

a second bite, while others are extremely poisonous and would kill most animals that consume a sufficient quantity. Unfortunately for the plants, most of these defenses are useless against their biggest

and their precious seeds are ready to be dispersed. Rain forest birds and mammals are vital agents in spreading seeds around, scattering them far and wide, along with a useful amount of ready-made fertilizer, in

*The tambaqui is one of many Amazonian fish that feed on fruits that fall into the water during the seasonal floods.*

*A strangler fig is beginning to encircle its host tree in a network of roots that will soon lead to its host's death.*

agents of dispersal are not monkeys or birds, but fish, which eagerly gather around the bases of some trees and gulp down the fruits as they fall into the water. Some of these fish feed on such huge quantities of fruits during the relatively short season that they put on enough extra weight to tide them over the long period of low water, when food is scarce.

Some of the most eagerly sought-after of the rain forest's delicacies are the fruits of strangler figs, which hang from the trees in great compact bunches. Strangler figs depend on the death of other trees for their success. A mighty strangler towering high above all its fellow trees will have begun life as a tiny seed that splattered in an animal dropping onto some branch high in the canopy. The germinating seedling survives initially as an epiphyte, but rapidly starts to send down long roots that eventually reach the ground. Once the roots are safely plugged into the nutrient cycle of the forest floor, they put on a spurt of growth and thicken rapidly, gradually wrapping the host tree's trunk in a strangling net. The host tree's stifled trunk eventually rots away, leaving its killer standing alone on its hollow latticework of a trunk.

their droppings. Many understory trees make life easier for animals to reach their fruits by arranging them neatly up the trunks or branches, rather than in hard-to-reach places at the tips of the twigs, as in most temperate forest trees. Cacao is a familar tree that flowers and fruits along the trunks and branches. In the flooded forests of Amazonia (the *igapo*) the trees drop their fruits into the water when the water levels are high. This might seem surprising, but in these forests the main

## Check these out:

● **Africa** ● **Asia** ● **Canopy** ● **Central America** ● **Climate and Weather** ● **Rain Forest** ● **Season** ● **South America**

Turtles are four-legged, slow-moving reptiles whose bodies are enclosed in a shell, called a carapace. They have scaly skin and lizardlike heads. They range in size from less than 4 inches (10 cm) to over 6½ feet (2 m). Aquatic species have limbs shaped like flippers for swimming, which they rotate in a figure-eight pattern as they swim. Many species have partially webbed feet. Freshwater turtles use their webbed hind feet as paddles. Terrapins—turtles that belong to the terrapin family (Emydidae)—are not very different from other turtles.

## KEY FACTS

● **Female snapping turtles can store a male's sperm for up to four years after mating, and still lay fertile eggs.**

● **The Southeast Asian leaf turtle looks just like a floating leaf. It has a flat, mottled shell with a wavy back edge.**

● **If threatened, turtles may hiss like snakes.**

● **A snapping turtle may travel up to 10 mi. (16 km) overland to reach its nesting site.**

Rain forests have plenty of small lakes, rivers, and streams that suit turtles and terrapins. Land-dwelling turtles, or tortoises, enjoy the dampness of the forest floor, with its rich insect life and tender young shoots. Some turtles, such as sliders, spend most of their lives in water, while others spend most of their time on land. Their diets range from vegetarian to carnivorous, and many will also scavenge for carrion (dead meat).

### The Protective Shell
The shell of a turtle is in two parts: an upper, often domed part, called the carapace, and a lower, usually flatter part, called the plastron. These parts are linked by bridges of shell between the front and

*A red–eared terrapin, or slider, basks on a rock. This is the most common species sold in the pet trade.*

# The Matamata Turtle

The well-camouflaged matamata turtle of South America has an extremely long snout. It stays submerged in shallow water, breathing through the snout's tip. Soft fleshy flaps on its chin alert it to movements in the water. This means it can hunt in murky water. The turtle waits until the prey comes within reach, then thrusts its head forward, opens its mouth, and lowers the floor of its large throat, sucking in its dinner.

hind limbs. The shell is made of an inner layer of fused plates of bones, covered by an outer layer made up of horny shields (scutes). A turtle's backbone is fused to its shell, providing extra support.

Just as in the skull of a human baby, the bony plates of a baby turtle's shell are not fused, but join up in a zigzag pattern of seams (sutures) as they knit together. In a few turtles, such as the African hingeback tortoise, the shell is hinged: a band of cartilage allows the tortoise to bend its

shell to enclose its hindquarters if it is in danger. The *Cuora* box turtles of Southeast Asia and the mud turtles of Central and South America have two hinges and can disappear completely inside their shells.

Most turtles can withdraw their heads and part of their limbs inside their shells. The sideneck or snake-necked turtles of South America, Africa, and Australia have long necks, which they draw sideways into their shells.

## Feeding Without Teeth

Turtles have no teeth. Instead, their horny jaws have sharp, often jagged edges. Turtles tend to tear at their food while holding it down with their feet. Vegetarian turtles feed on the softest parts of plants, while predatory turtles, such as mud turtles, eat worms, snails, slugs, insects, and shellfish. A few of the larger turtles, such as the snapping turtle of Central America and the United States, can catch fish.

## Living in Water

Turtles do not breathe like humans do. Their ribs cannot move within the shell to draw in breaths, so they have to pump air into their lungs with their throats. This also draws smells past the smell-sensing part of the snout. Many aquatic turtles, such as the softshells of Africa and Asia, gain extra oxygen by sucking water into their mouths and extracting oxygen from

## IN FOCUS

# Protecting Nesting Sites

Some aquatic turtles, such as the South American arau river turtle, migrate along rivers to lay their eggs together on the same favorite sandbar. All the turtles of a particular area lay their eggs in the same place. On Venezuela's Orinoco beach, 123,600 turtles nested in 1945. Unfortunately so many eggs were taken for food that by 1969 only 13,800 turtles turned up to lay. Now more nest sites are protected and the turtles are recovering their numbers.

it as it passes over the lining of the mouth. Some take it in through the mouth and expel it through their nostrils, while others do the opposite. Softshells also have a lighter shell, which makes it easier for them to maintain their positions in the water, since they are less likely to keep sinking.

## Reproduction

Turtle courtship is usually a chase and charge affair. The male pursues the female until she stops, then lunges at her, pushing her around and biting her legs until she agrees to mate.

*A scorpion mud turtle roams the rain forest floor of Selva Verde, Costa Rica.*

*A baby Chinese box turtle hatches from its shell. The eggs have incubated in a damp corner of the forest floor.*

Turtles lay from one egg to 200 eggs at a time, usually in a pit in sand or soil, but sometimes on damp ground, hidden among leaves. After laying their eggs, they abandon them to develop alone.

When a baby turtle hatches, it has a horny toothlike structure on its snout to cut through the eggshell. This falls off after the turtle hatches. Turtles take several years to become mature enough to breed—some musk turtles take 11 years— but most turtles are very long-lived, often living beyond 20 years and sometimes much longer.

**Trading in Turtles**

Humans have enjoyed the taste of turtles and their eggs for thousands of years. In many places where large numbers of eggs are taken each year, the turtles are at risk of dying out.

In recent years turtles and terrapins have become popular pets. Turtle farms have been set up in the United States and Malaysia to raise turtles for the pet markets. The commonest species raised for the pet trade is the red-eared slider. Turtles that have been introduced from other countries are sometimes released by pet owners when they get too big. They can then cause damage to local animals and waterways.

## Check these out:
● **Endangered Species** ● Reptile

Much of what goes on in the rain forest takes place way up out of sight, in the sun-drenched canopy. Many animals, such as most monkeys and sloths, rarely venture out of it. Down below, between the canopy and the ground, lies the understory, with its tangle of vines and lianas (lee-AH-nuhs) snaking their way up into the treetops.

## KEY FACTS

● As little as one percent of the sunlight falling on the canopy will reach the forest floor.

● Spiders are more abundant in the understory than in the canopy.

● Some monkeys prefer the understory because they feed mainly on palm fruits.

The understory is quite different from the world above. For a start, so much of the bright tropical sunlight is filtered out by the millions of intervening leaves that only a tiny fraction reaches the ground. This makes the understory permanently gloomy and pleasantly cool. Walking through the forest can be surprisingly easy, because the interior is often quite lofty and open, with no need to hack a path with a machete, as so often seen in movies.

### Plants of the Understory

This lower level of the forest is often dominated by palms, which are small trees with fanlike leaves. The trunks of many rain forest palms are covered with long spines. These trunks may be supported by a mass of stiltlike roots, which help anchor them in the thin soil. This extra support protects the trees from one of the common hazards facing any of the smaller trees in the rain forest, which is to be knocked over by a much larger tree during a rainstorm. When a rain forest giant falls, it brings dozens of smaller trees with it.

*Palms, like those seen here against a mist-filled sky in Venezuela, are very common in the understory.*

590

*The bright red flowers of crab claw plants are common in the understory of Central and South American rain forests.*

Plants with oversize leaves are characteristic of the understory. In Central and South America, many parts of the understory are dominated by dense and colorful groves of heliconia flowers, also called crab claws. They have long leaves, similar to those of the banana tree, and spikes of brilliant red, yellow, and pink flowers, eagerly visited by hungry hummingbirds. The leaves are eaten by the giant horned caterpillars of owl butterflies, which are among the world's biggest butterflies. Wasps like to attach their paper nests to the undersides of the broad leaves, which keep out the rain. One plant which has some of the broadest leaves of all is the elephant's ears. It has a large bulbous root (called a corm), which is made into flour by local people.

One family of plants typical of the ground-level section of the understory is the gingers, which often form dense headhigh stands. Their flowers are some of the most brilliantly conspicuous of the gloomy rain forest interior; some species produce their blooms right on the ground.

In Central and South America the pervading green of the forest floor is often broken by bright splashes of red. These are hot-lips flowers, which resemble a pair of lips generously smeared with glossy red or purple lipstick.

Many familar houseplants, with their broad green leathery leaves, come from the permanently shady understory, which is why they can live and grow quite happily indoors, well away from any window. Among these are the dumbcanes (dieffenbachias), with their large glossy tufts of leaves; the anthuriums, with their strange hooded jack-in-the-pulpit flowers; and the Swiss-cheese plants (monsteras), easily recognized by their leaves, which are full of large holes. In their forest homes many of these grow in a coiled tangle, looping their way up into the canopy.

## IN FOCUS

## Light Gaps

Where the understory is dense and there are no light gaps, animal life can be quite scarce. Insects are rare, although certain butterflies prefer the cool, gloomy understory. Where a tree has fallen and light has flooded in, a transformation takes place. There is a rapid surge of plant growth, accompanied by hordes of insects such as butterflies, bugs, and beetles. The same effect can be seen where the forest is penetrated by a broad track, whose sunlit edges will attract masses of insects.

## Check these out:
- Canopy ● Flowering Plant ● Leaf
- ● Light Gap ● Palm Tree ● Photosynthesis
- ● Plant ● Rain Forest ● Shade Toleration

A vertebrate is any animal that has a backbone, or spine. The hard, bony skeleton lies on the inside, forming a strong and rigid internal framework that supports all the soft parts—skin, muscle, heart, lungs, kidneys, liver, etc. In contrast, invertebrate animals (such as insects, crabs, millipedes, and spiders) have no internal skeletons, but they usually have a relatively tough skeleton on the outside. This forms a complete outer cage with all the softer parts protected on the inside, like in a can.

Vertebrate animals are divided into five main groupings, namely fish, amphibians, reptiles, birds, and mammals. All of these types are well represented in the rain forest, which is home to more different species of vertebrates than any other nonmarine habitat.

## KEY FACTS

● Poisonous snakes inject venom through a pair of hollow fangs.

● Most birds have hollow bones. This makes them light and enables them to fly more easily.

● Many mammals pant, rather than sweat, to keep cool.

## Fish

Fish obviously look very different from any land-living animals, and this is reflected in the way they behave. The most obvious difference is that most fish breathe water instead of air, so they usually have no lungs. Instead, water is forced through their gills, which are designed to maximize the amount of oxygen that is extracted from the water. A few fish have lungs or breathe largely through their skins.

## RAIN FOREST VERTEBRATES

Mudskipper

Manatee

Poison Dart Frog

## Frog Orgies

In some frogs and toads the tadpoles develop within the mother's body, while in others, such as many poison dart frogs, they are carried on the back of the adult frog. Some rain forest frogs, such as the harlequin-patterned tree frog from Central America, are so-called explosive breeders. This means that they all pair up and lay eggs in a great orgy, which lasts just a few hectic hours on a single night, usually after a spell of heavy rain has broken a drier period. Amphibians are among the noisiest of all the rain forest's inhabitants, calling loudly at night (and also sometimes by day) to attract mates. Some of the tiniest frogs produce a truly astonishing volume of sound, often a very birdlike chirp.

The Amazon rain forest has more fish than the rest of the world's freshwater systems added together, with over 5,000 species. Some of these are quite unusual, such as the electric eel that can stun its prey with a high-voltage discharge and the stingray that can maim a person with the powerful toxic sting in its spiny whiplash tail. Some of the most colorful and highly prized aquarium fish come from rain forest rivers, especially the multicolored neons and guppies from the rivers of South America.

**Amphibians**

Amphibians include caecilians (sih-SIHL-yuhns), newts, salamanders, frogs, and toads. Caecilians are wormlike creatures that live in burrows and are rarely seen. Newts and salamanders are far more common in temperate northern areas than in the Tropics. Only the young stages of amphibians live in water, although even this has been dispensed with in some frogs and toads. Amphibians generally have very soft, moist skin that easily loses water. Although some species are highly adapted for living in dry places, most of

Green Day Gecko

Common Vampire Bat

Military Macaw

the nearly 3,500 species that have been named so far live in a permanently humid environment. It is not surprising that the bulk of these are found in wet tropical rain forests. Many species of frogs in this constantly damp habitat have evolved to the point where they no longer need water for a tadpole stage. Instead, perfectly formed froglets emerge from extra-large eggs laid in some dripping-wet nook in the rain forest itself.

## Reptiles

Reptiles include tortoises and terrapins, lizards, snakes, and crocodilians. All of these are common in rain forests. There are more than 6,500 different species of reptiles around the world. The most prominent reptiles in most rain forests are lizards. The key to the reptiles' ability to live in many different habitats lies in their skin, which is much thicker than that of amphibians. It is composed of thousands of tiny overlapping scales that are good for retaining water inside the body. Most reptiles lay eggs, although a few lizards and numerous snakes give birth to live young. Reptiles are cold-blooded; they regulate their body temperatures by basking in the sun, although this is not as necessary in warm tropical rain forests. Some lizards are legless and look like snakes. Many of the rain forest snakes live up in the trees rather than on the ground. Long and whiplike, they slide easily through the tangle of lianas (lee-AH-nuhs) and vines, where they are very hard to see.

*Manakins are typical birds of the rain forests of Central and South America. This is a male red-capped manakin from Panama.*

## Birds

Birds are characterized by their ability to fly, though a few are flightless. Flightless rain forest species include the cassowary of Australia and New Guinea and the kiwi of New Zealand's temperate rain forests. A bird's most prominent feature is its feathers, which in many tropical species are brightly colored. Birds have no hands, so the beak does most of the work of handling food and preening feathers. Beaks come in a variety of shapes and sizes, adapted for particular types of food. A toucan's long, bulbous but very lightweight beak is designed for reaching across to grasp fruits on slender twigs that would not support the bird's weight. A sunbird's long, thin, downcurved beak is designed for probing flowers for nectar; the beaks of the rain forest hawks and eagles are sharply hooked at the tip for tearing flesh apart.

Unlike reptiles, birds are warm-blooded, although they will often bask in the sun on a cool morning.

# Tenrecs

Madagascar is home to one of the strangest families of rain forest mammals, the tenrecs. Tenrecs resemble miniature porcupines and often have similar habits, sniffing on the ground for insects and other invertebrates. They may travel in large family groups, nose to tail, in long processions.

All birds lay eggs: there are none that give birth to live young. Birds are divided into numerous families, many of which are most abundant in rain forests, such as the tanagers, manakins, pittas, turacos, antshrikes, broadbills, and jacamars.

## Mammals

Except for many squirrels and primates, most rain forest mammals are active only at night, so are rarely seen. Mammals are covered with fur or hair rather than feathers, and like birds they are warm-blooded. Mammals have adapted to most environments on land, sea, and air. Examples of all these adaptations are found in rain forests, such as hoofed animals, cats, and primates on land;

porpoises, otters, manatees, and dolphins in some of the major rivers; and hordes of bats in the skies. Bats are the only mammals that have mastered true flight, although the rain forests are home to several kinds of gliders, including the flying squirrels and flying lemur.

Mammals generally give birth to live young, although a small number of very primitive Australian species still lay eggs. Even these feed their offspring on milk, produced within the mother's body. In marsupials (such as kangaroos and possums) the young are born at a very immature stage and complete their development within a pouch on the mother's belly. In placental mammals, the young are born in a more fully developed state and can sometimes even walk and run within minutes of being born.

Most adult mammals have teeth. In some families of mammals, such as rodents, the teeth grow continuously throughout life, so they have to be kept in check by regular gnawing on some hard substance, such as wood.

## Check these out:
● Amphibian ● Bird ● Fish ● Frog and Toad ● Lizard ● Mammal ● Possum ● Reptile ● Rodent ● Snake ● Toucan

Vultures are birds that feed mainly on corpses and are often the first scavengers to move in on a dead animal. They tear it apart, plunging their heads into the carcass to reach the choicest morsels. This makes it easier for smaller scavengers to break the corpse down further, releasing its nutrients.

Armed with hooked bills for tearing flesh, vultures have long necks for reaching inside carcasses. Their heads and necks are often bare of feathers, which prevents them from getting too messy while feeding.

## Hunting Using Smell

Normally vultures hunt from high in the sky, soaring and gliding on their long, outstretched wings. Vultures that scavenge in the rain forest, however, are not able to spot food from the sky, because they cannot see through the canopy. Instead, the vultures of North and South America, especially the king vulture and the turkey vulture, have a well-developed sense of smell.

The highly adaptable turkey vulture lives in a wide range of habitats, from the cold deserts of Patagonia to the tropical rain forests and even to southern Canada. Unlike other vultures, its wings are raised at an angle when gliding, and it tilts from side to side as it flies. When seeking food it flies low over the ground, picking up smells as it goes.

The king vulture of the tropical Americas is the most colorful of them all, with its striking red, orange, and blue head. Most vultures live in groups, but the king vulture lives alone, soaring high over the forest until its keen sense of smell detects a corpse. Other vultures, such as the Asian king vulture, sometimes hunt in dense forest, but they rely more on sight than smell to find their food.

An unusual species is the palm-nut vulture of African mangrove swamps and palm plantations. This vulture is mostly vegetarian, feeding primarily on the husks of oil palms, supplemented by small fish, crabs, frogs, and invertebrates.

*The king vulture is one of the few birds with a keen sense of smell.*

## Check these out:
- Bird ● Decomposer
- Food Web

# Water

In the early morning a mist appears to curl up out of the rain forest, drifting over the canopy in swirls. Yet in the shade below, the air is clear. The mist appears to be coming from the canopy itself, and in a way it is. The sun is warming the whole forest, and the warm, moist air trapped below the canopy rises and escapes. Above the canopy it meets cooler air, so the moisture in it condenses to form mist. Within an hour the mist has gone as more air warms up.

A rain forest acts like a giant sponge. There is very little runoff from a rain forest. The rain trickles slowly down though the layers of dense vegetation, some of it evaporating on the way. It then seeps through the leaves on the forest floor and into the soil, where much of it is again taken up by the dense mat of roots. Up to 95 percent of the annual rainfall may be retained in this root network.

*Early morning mist bathes the cloud forest of Venezuela. Warm air rising through the moist forest meets cooler air above, and its moisture condenses to form clouds.*

Water taken up by the roots rises through the trees to evaporate again from the canopy. Some sinks down through the soil and drains into rivers, but it takes a long time. Consequently, rain forests can help keep rivers flowing even when there is no rainfall—they can affect the water supply of regions thousands of miles away. Rain forest can absorb up to 120 inches (3,000 mm) of rainfall a year, helping to regulate the water supply of millions of people downstream and downwind.

## The Water Cycle

Almost 50 percent of the rain falling over the Amazon basin is recycled to the atmosphere by the forest. The rest trickles slowly down through the foliage and into the soil, where it drains into rivers. Evaporation from the ground and from leaf surfaces is the main way in which water reaches the atmosphere. In a rain forest, it evaporates from the leaves until the air is almost saturated. In the heat of the afternoon, so much evaporation is

*The rains arrive at an area of forest in the upper Amazon River basin. Soon the forest will be flooded, and fish will move in to feed and breed.*

taking place that huge clouds billow above the forest, discharging their contents amid bursts of thunder and lightning.

The clouds drift on the wind, so this cycle of evaporation and precipitation gradually moves the water farther and farther downwind, often to areas that would otherwise receive very little rainfall—areas that would be seriously affected if the rain forest were destroyed. Studies in Brazil show that 20 percent less water evaporates from cleared land than from forests.

Where there is not such thick vegetation—in cleared areas or farmland—more of the water that falls on the land runs straight into rivers. In areas of heavy rainfall, the runoff may carry with it valuable topsoil. This runoff may lead to flooding as the volume of water increases and the rivers silt up with soil.

## Water Everywhere

The constantly moist environment of the rain forest allows animals with thin, moist skin, such as frogs and salamanders, to live away from rivers and ponds. Flatworms and leeches slither over leaves,

*This tiny salamander is living in a bromeliad high up in the canopy. It will lay its eggs and rear its young in this private pool.*

and worms can be found hundreds of feet above the ground in the piles of leaf debris that accumulate around epiphytic plants.

Tiny pools of water collect in the centers of such plants as bromeliads (broe-MEE-lee-ads), between the fronds of epiphytic ferns, and in the pitchers of carnivorous plants. These are home to many aquatic creatures such as frogs, mosquitoes, damselflies, salamanders, and even crabs. There are land-dwelling crabs in many rain forests. They need water to rear their young, so they lay their eggs in these tiny pools. The pools do not contain enough food for the young, so the parent crabs bring food to them.

Tadpoles also live in these pools. With enemies like dragonfly larvae around, it is not safe to lay eggs there, so the frogs lay their eggs in moist crannies, then carry their tadpoles to water. These tiny pools are like miniature water holes, attracting many small creatures to drink or to hunt.

**Waterways Under Threat**

With the increasing felling of forests for commerce or cultivation, the rain forest rivers are under threat. In the Ivory Coast, West Africa, the annual loss of soil from the forest slopes was estimated at 165 lbs per acre (30 kg per hectare) per year. From an unforested slope it was an amazing 121 tons per acre (138 tonnes per hectare) a year. Increased soil erosion silts up rivers and cuts out the light to aquatic plants. High rates of runoff and flash floods may sweep away fish that would normally graze on flooded meadows. The floods undercut banks, causing forest trees to fall into the water.

In many parts of the Tropics, mining operations discharge dangerous heavy metals into the rivers, poisoning animals and people far downstream. Gold mining is particularly disasterous. The (often illegal) miners use mercury, a fatal toxin, to extract the gold.

## IN FOCUS

### The Panama Canal

In the late 1970s the level of water in the Panama Canal dropped dramatically. The cause was thought to be destruction of the rain forests on the surrounding hills. Without the forests, there was a less steady supply of water, and worse still, soil erosion was silting up the canal. In 1983 the government introduced strict laws against logging.

## Check these out:

- Climate and Weather   ● Flooding   ● River
- Season   ● Watershed

A watershed is an area that drains away rainfall via a particular set of streams and rivers. A watershed is separated from neighboring ones by ridges along hills or mountains. Any rain or melting snow falling in this area will soak into the surrounding soil, which acts as a sponge and regulates the rate at which water drains off the land and into the streams and rivers. A watershed can be tiny, such as one that covers the runoff into a pond, or enormous, such as the Amazon River and all its tributaries. The Amazon, in fact, is formed from the watersheds of its tributaries in the Andes Mountains as well as from the watershed formed by the rain forest of the Amazon River basin itself.

## KEY FACTS

● **Watersheds act as an important store of water, releasing it only gradually.**

● **Damage to a watershed can have far-reaching consequences on its river system.**

### Feeding the Forest

Watersheds are important for rain forests for many different reasons. Water that filters down from watersheds can bring vital nutrients to the growing forest. Some of the water in the rivers that run through much of the world's rain forest has come down from hills and mountain ranges on which the rain has fallen. This water will contain minerals it has dissolved out of the rocks. Some rocks will be rich in these minerals, while others will release little into the water passing over them. Since at certain times many of the rivers flood into the rain forest farther down, the quantity of mineral nutrients for plant growth flowing into the forest will depend on the watershed from which the river flows.

### Regulating Water Supplies

Watersheds are also very effective reservoirs. During periods of very heavy rainfall, they soak up the water and release it into the rivers in a controlled fashion. In this way they may prevent a river from flooding or from drying up during the dry season. Any damage to a watershed can, therefore, have widespread and long-lasting consequences. In the last few decades a great deal of felling has taken place in watershed forests, and the results have been alarming. With the removal

*Running through a steep-sided valley in Peru is a tributary stream of the Ucayali River, which eventually flows into the Amazon River.*

### A RAIN FOREST WATERSHED

of vegetation and its roots, the soils become unstable, and during heavy rain they are washed into the rivers, which become heavily silted. This silt is then washed downstream, where it can have disastrous effects on modern hydroelectric systems. Water from behind a dam falls through huge pipes and drives a series of turbines, generating electricity.

*Rain falling on hills and mountains filters down to the forest below, which retains some of the water like a sponge.*

The silt builds up behind the dams, blocking these pipes, and enormously expensive projects become totally useless.

Even more unpleasant can be the effects of heavy rain on local people. Water that was once held by the soils of the watershed now runs off very rapidly, causing rock and mud slides that can sweep away people and their homes. Rivers also flood much more quickly, with devastating results. If the watershed is completely cleared and all of the topsoil is washed away, the final result can be a desert, where virtually nothing will ever grow again.

## IN FOCUS

## Siltation

When watershed forest is cut down and erosion increases, great quantities of silt are released into the rivers. This can eventually make its way down to the sea. The silt may then be washed along the coast by coastal currents and can end up being deposited on coral reefs. The silt clogs up the coral, which then dies, and as a result the whole reef and its associated wildlife may be destroyed.

## Check these out:
● Erosion ● Flooding ● Hydroelectricity
● National Park ● River ● Water

# Worm

The name *worm* is given to various slender-bodied invertebrates belonging to several very different groups. The length of these creatures is usually many times the width, and most of them lack any kind of limbs. The most familiar worms are the annelids, whose bodies are divided into numerous rings or segments. They include earthworms, leeches, and numerous marine forms called bristleworms.

## KEY FACTS

● **Earthworms over 6 ft. (2 m) long can be found in several parts of the world.**

● **Earthworms have no eyes, but they always try to move away from the light.**

● **All earthworms and leeches have both male and female parts, but the worms still need to pair up and mate before they can lay eggs.**

## Earthworms Almost Everywhere

Earthworms spend most of their time tunneling through soil. They swallow a lot of soil as they go and digest any animal and vegetable matter in it. Undigested material is passed out in the form of worm casts on or near the surface. The worms move with the aid of tiny bristles borne on the lower surface of the body. With the rear end firmly anchored to the tunnel walls by the bristles, the worm stretches forward and anchors its front end, then uses powerful muscles to pull the rest of its body forward.

Though they live in nearly every kind of soil, earthworms do not like very dry or acidic soils. It was once thought that earthworms were not common in the rain forests because there are so many ants and termites living in the soil, but recent studies have shown that this is not true. Earthworm populations in rain forests are not much different from those in temperate woodlands, although the species are not the same. In several rain forest areas, earthworms account for just over half the total weight of soil animals. Termites come next, with about one-eighth of the total animal weight.

The rain forest soils of any particular area may contain 10 or 12 species, belonging to three ecological groups. The fairly small, dark worms that wander freely through the leaf litter, eating it as they go, are called epigeic (eh-pih-JEE-ik) worms.

*The bright colors of this flatworm crawling over the forest floor suggest that it has an unpleasant taste.*

*This large orange-and-black flatworm has captured a snail. The flatworm will pour digestive juices over it and suck up the resulting solution.*

divided into segments. It has numerous short legs—more than 40 pairs in some species—and a pair of antennae. About 100 different species, ranging from half an inch (1 cm) to 6 inches (15 cm) in length, are distributed across the warmer parts of the world. Most of them live in the rain forests, where they eat termites, snails, and other soft-bodied animals.

The much larger species that live in permanent vertical burrows are called anecic (an-EE-sik) worms. Both groups play a major role in removing dead leaves from the forest floor. The pale, medium-sized species that live deeper in the soil and feed on much smaller particles of decaying matter are called endogeic (en-doe-JEE-ik) worms.

## Colorful Flatworms

Flatworms are often mistaken for small black leeches. Most are aquatic creatures, but many thrive in the rain forests at all levels, from the floor to the canopy. They glide over the ever-present film of water with the aid of minute hairs called cilia. Some forest flatworms are quite broad and resemble colorful leaves. They all feed on other animals, but they can go without food for months, during which time they digest parts of their own bodies and become even thinner than they normally are.

## Velvet Worms

Named for its soft, velvety skin, a velvet worm looks like a cross between an earthworm and a caterpillar. It has a wormlike body, although it is not clearly

### IN FOCUS

## Clinging Leeches

Most leeches live in ponds and streams, but the rain forests are wet enough for some species to survive on land. They have no bristles, but move over the ground or the vegetation with the aid of a sucker at each end. Many species eat other small, soft-bodied animals, but some are specialized blood-feeders. The front sucker surrounds a cluster of sharp teeth that cut into the flesh of the victim. Then the leech sucks up the blood. When it is full, it drops off to digest its meal. Some leeches can soak up more than their own weight of blood at a single meal. People walking through rain forest vegetation often find small leeches attached to them.

## Check these out:

- Decomposer ● Forest Floor
- Invertebrate ● Leech ● Locomotion

# Yanomami People

The Yanomami (ee-on-oe-MA-mee), also called Yanomani and Yanomamo, are a native people of the tropical rain forests of Brazil and Venezuela in South America. They live along the border of those two countries in one of the most remote parts of the continent.

In Venezuela their land lies along the headwaters of the Orinoco River, while in Brazil they are located along the headwaters of some of the northern tributaries of the Amazon River. Their total population is estimated at about 20,000.

The remoteness of their land kept them in isolation from the outside world until the 20th century. They are today the largest remaining remote group of native people in South America.

## KEY FACTS

● There are about 20,000 Yanomami people living in Venezuela and Brazil.

● The Yanomami are the largest remaining remote group of native people in the Amazon rain forest.

● Yanomami land is being overrun by gold miners, who have brought diseases and destroyed the environment.

## A Yanomami Village

The Yanomami live in more than one hundred villages throughout their land. The villages are made up of one huge circular building with a large opening in the center of the roof for an open-air courtyard. Each family is responsible for constructing its portion of the building and roof.

The villages are more permanent sites than those of many other rain forest people. This is because the Yanomami are able to practice slash-and-burn agriculture at different sites near the village for a long time. To harvest the seasonal wild forest crops, they will make trips lasting a day or two from the village.

*Yanomami hunters like this one share whatever they kill with other hunters.*

## IN FOCUS

# Sharing the Hunt

Generosity is a highly prized trait among the Yanomami: they believe it is the most important thing for which a person's life will be judged when they die. A Yanomami hunter gives away all the meat from an animal he has killed. He believes if he eats the meat himself, he will offend the spirit of the animal. He relies on the generosity of other hunters to give him a portion of their meat.

Each village has long-standing formal trade relations with several other villages. However, the Yanomami also have a long-standing tradition of raiding other villages, especially for wives.

These different relationships, one peaceful and one violent, make the Yanomami villagers very cautious in their dealings with one another. A visit by one village to another for a peaceful purpose, such as a feast, is done with great ceremony and caution.

## Modern-Day Threats

The Yanomami were mostly left alone until a gold rush began in their country in 1990. In a short time thousands of gold hunters poured in. Armed and dangerous, with no regard for the native people or the environment, the gold hunters created havoc. They destroyed streambeds with high-pressure water hoses. They poisoned rivers with deadly mercury used in the gold separation process. They killed Yanomamis, sometimes entire villages; and they brought diseases.

The plight of the Yanomamis soon became known throughout the world. Human rights groups began pressuring Brazil and Venezuela to save the Yanomami. Yanomami leaders, such as Dani Yanomami, became well-known speakers for their people.

The governments of Brazil and Venezuela have sometimes responded to the pressure by announcing measures to help the Yanomami. At other times the governments continue to pursue policies that open the rain forest to exploitation and destruction. No one knows if the Yanomami will be able to survive the gold rush.

*Yanomami children dance in a village clearing.*

## Check these out:

● Homes in the Rain Forest ● Hunter-Gatherer ● People of the Rain Forest

# Glossary

**Aboriginal:** the original inhabitants of a country. Used especially for the original inhabitants of Australia.

**Aroid:** a large family of plants with broad, glossy, deep green leaves, many of which occur in the rain forest understory.

**Bromeliad:** any of over one thousand plants of the pineapple family with a crown of stiff, spiny leaves. Some bromeliads grow on the ground, but most of them perch on trees.

**Cartilage:** a dense tissue that covers the surfaces of bones at the joints, protecting them from being damaged by rubbing against each other.

**Cataract:** a waterfall.

**Cellulose:** the main building material of the plant kingdom. It is present in all cell walls and in most of the tough fibers in stems and leaves.

**Ecosystem:** a group of plants and animals that interact with each other in an area (called their environment). A single tree and a whole forest are both ecosystems.

**Epiphyte:** any plant that grows on another without taking food from it. Most epiphytes grow on trees.

**Evaporation:** the process by which a liquid turns into a vapor (gas).

**Exoskeleton:** a hard outer covering that protects the soft bodies of invertebrates such as insects, spiders, crustaceans, and shellfish.

**Fauna:** animal life.

**Feral:** a wild animal that is descended from domestic animals.

**Germinate:** to begin to grow, as when a seed produces roots and shoots.

**Humus:** compost of decayed vegetable matter occurring as a component of soils on the surface of the ground.

**Invertebrate:** an animal that lacks a spinal column (backbone). Invertebrates have no bony skeletons. They may have a hard outer shell, like insects, or soft bodies supported by water pressure, as in worms.

**Larva:** the stage of an invertebrate's life between the egg and the adult.

**Liana:** a climbing plant with long tendrils that grows up trees to reach sunlight.

**Monsoon:** a wind, mainly in southern Asia, that blows toward the land in summer, bringing a deluge of rain.

**Nitrate:** mineral salt that contains nitrogen and oxygen. Nitrates are soluble in water, so they are important sources of nitrogen for plants.

**Phosphate:** mineral compounds that contain phosphorus and oxygen, derived from the breakdown of rocks to form soil. Phosphates are involved in the energy-generating processes of all living things and form many substances in cells.

**Photosynthesis:** the process by which green plants and some algae and bacteria use the energy of sunlight to build up chemical compounds (foods) from carbon dioxide and water. Photosynthesizing plants give off oxygen as a by-product.

**Placental:** describing mammals that give birth to relatively well-developed young. The placenta is an organ that attaches the developing baby to the inside of the mother.

**Prehensile:** a limb that can grasp objects.

**Primate:** an animal of the family of apes and monkeys, including humans.

**Quassia:** a tree that produces a bitter medicinal tonic and insecticide.

**Rheumatism:** a severe inflammation of the joints and muscles that causes stiffness and pain.

**Silt:** particles of rock and soil that are washed into streams and rivers during heavy rainfall.

**Subtropical:** areas with a tropical climate and habitat but lying just outside the Tropics, i.e., north of the tropic of Cancer and south of the tropic of Capricorn.

**Tannins:** defensive bitter chemicals found in the bark, leaves, and fruits of many rain forest trees.

**Temperate rain forest:** high rainfall forest in the temperate regions of the world with a distinct winter and summer.

**Topsoil:** the upper layers and surface of the soil, in which plants take root.

**Tributary:** a small stream or river that flows into a larger stream or river.

**Tropics:** the area of the earth's surface between the tropic of Cancer and the tropic of Capricorn, on either side of the equator, at which the sun can be directly overhead, resulting in high average temperatures year round.

**Understory:** the layer of trees and shrubs between the forest floor and the canopy.

**Vertebrate:** any animal that possesses a backbone, e.g., fish, amphibians, reptiles, birds, and mammals.

# Index

29081

10 9 8 7 6 5 4 3 2 1

Library of Congress Cataloging-in-Publication Data

Davis, Maggie S.. 1942 — The rinky-dink cafe / by Maggie S. Davis. p. cm. Summary: An
insatiable pig marches into a restaurant that advertises "Dinners Made to Order" and demands
an amazing and amusing variety of dishes. ISBN 0-671-66408-5 [1. Pigs — Fiction. 2.
Food — Fiction.] I. Title. PZ7.D2952R in   1988 [E] — dc19   87-35435   CIP   AC

For my mother
M.S.D.

Made to order for
Rick and Deann
J.S.

The
# Rinky-dink
Café

By
Maggie S. Davis

Illustrated by
John Sandford

Simon and Schuster Books for Young Readers    Published by Simon & Schuster Inc.

New York

Into the Rinky-dink Café
marched Piggy La Puffin on Thanksgiving Day.
Cook waved from the kitchen. Waitress did, too.
"Have a seat," they called sweetly. "We're tasting a stew."

Piggy sat. Then she saw—in a crooked black border—
a large sign that read: WE MAKE DINNERS TO ORDER.

"It's true," grinned the waitress. "Ah," Piggy sighed.
"Then bring me cod soup and hot cider," she cried,
"and a bucket of clams caught near Old Plymouth Rock.
Could you serve up the clams in a pumpkin-shaped crock?"
"Don't know," said the waitress. "I'll go and ask Cook."
And ask him she did.

Well, Cook flashed a look that made poor Waitress fret.
His face was as gloomy as faces can get.
"I'm feeling blue," he moaned, checking the order.
"Darn that old sign with the crooked black border!"

"Something else?" asked the waitress. "You bet," Piggy said.
"A platter of oysters and fresh homebaked bread.
Some sliced beef with mustard, plus grapes—just a tad—
and corn that was picked by an Indian lad.
Serve it all on a garland of red and gold leaves.
Then, of course, a container of bread pudding, please."
"*My, my!*" said the waitress. "I'll go and tell Cook."
And tell him she did.

Well, Cook flashed a look that made poor Waitress dizzy.
He rolled and he bounced and he flew in a tizzy.
"I'm feeling weird," he wailed, waving the order.
"Let's rip up that sign with the crooked black border!"

"Something else?" asked the waitress, hefting the food.
"Right you are," Piggy said, " 'cause I'm in the mood
for sizzling plum porridge and turkey and dressing
and turnips and dumplings—I know I'm just guessing,
but do you have apples and steaming mince pies
that were baked by a child who can cross both his eyes?
Barrels of cranberries—that would be dandy—
and armfuls of cherries, and trays of nut candy,
and—"
"Stop!" said the waitress. "I'll go and tell Cook."
And tell him she did.

Well, Cook flashed a look that made poor Waitress sick.
He turned rosy red, beat the air with a stick.
"I'm feeling fierce!" he shrieked, spearing the order.
"I'll *eat* that old sign with the crooked black border!"

From the kitchen came shouts of "I wish I were dead!"
Piggy ignored them. She hummed and she read.
Waitress came out. Steam rose from her wig.
She looked older and wilder. "You ungrateful pig!"
were the words that she said as she wielded her tray.
"Could you bring me more food?" Piggy asked. "Right away?"

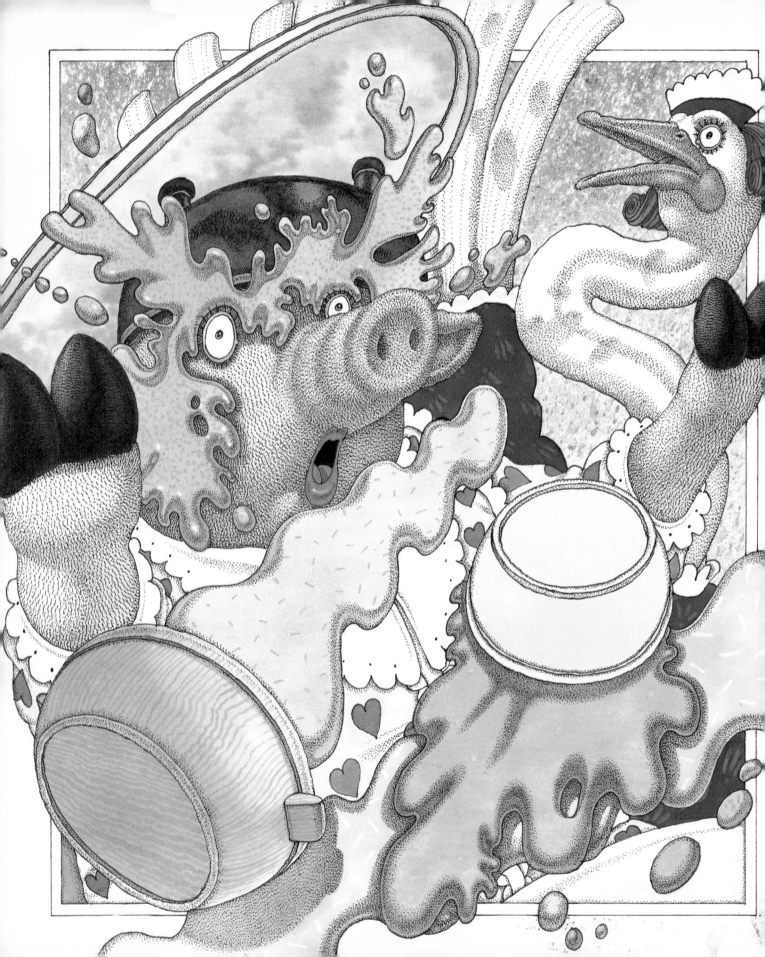

Just at that moment a shocking surprise—
the tray teetertottered. Despite Piggy's cries,
huge pots of goop tumbled down on her head.
When Piggy complained, Waitress scowled and she said:

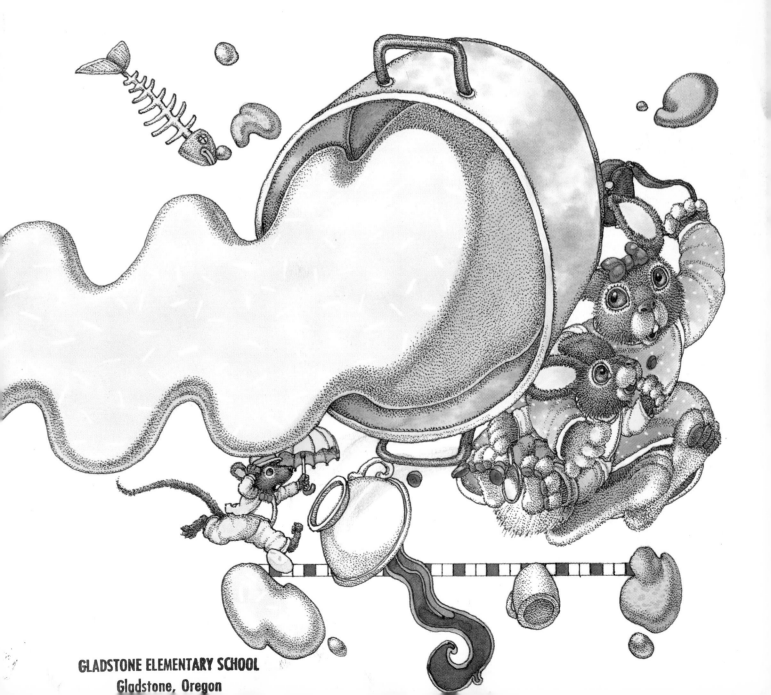

"I'll forget that our restaurant is  flooded with trash.
I'll forget you owe Cook and me buckets of cash.
I'll forget you aged each of us forty-three years,
that our Thanksgiving customers left here in tears.
But if you want sand that a pilgrim child played in,
more turkey, more cider, or even one raisin,
do not come to me with what you're proposing.
I'm pooped. Cook's on strike. What's more, dearie, we're *closing!*"

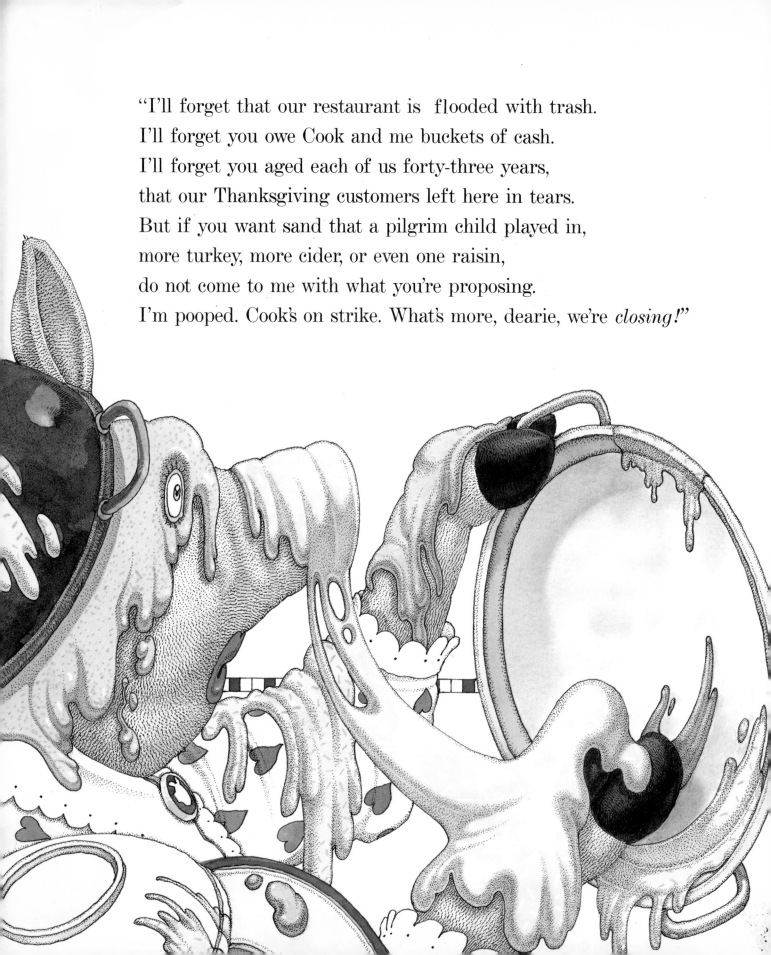

"Hmm," Piggy said, "I enjoyed your fine dinner
but dare say, I'm stuck here till I can get thinner."
Well, Waitress saw stars— couldn't take any more.
She called Cook: "Let's try pushing that pig out the door!"
"Whoa!" Piggy said. "I know what I'll do.
While I'm getting thin, I'll fix dinner for you!"
Waitress was tickled. Cook seemed pleased, too.
They waited politely till Piggy was through.

Then they ate every morsel she put on their plates.

Piggy tidied and scrubbed. In no time, she'd lost weight.

"Oh, thank you," Cook trilled. "We loved our Thanksgiving, dear—"
"Me, too!" said Piggy. "I'll come back next year!"